FOOD
and FIRE

MARCUS BAWDON

FOOD
and FIRE

CREATE BOLD DISHES
WITH **65** RECIPES TO
COOK OUTDOORS

DOG 'N' BONE

Published in 2019 by Dog 'n' Bone Books
An imprint of Ryland Peters & Small Ltd
20–21 Jockey's Fields   341 E 116th St
London WC1R 4BW   New York,
                                          NY 10029

www.rylandpeters.com

10 9 8 7 6

A CIP catalog record for this book is available
from the Library of Congress and the British
Library.

ISBN: 978 1 911026 88 4

Printed in China

Editor: Caroline West
Designer: Eoghan O'Brien
Photographer: Marcus Bawdon
Additional photography: Matt Austin (pages
14, 19, 20, 36, 51, 63 bottom and right, 90,
129, back cover), Nick Hook, and Richard
Budd (page 2)
Illustrator: Chris Ledward

CONTENTS

INTRODUCTION

1
DIRTY

2
CAMPFIRES AND FIREPITS

3
CAST-IRON COOKING

INTRODUCTION

IF YOU ARE NEAR A FIRE, YOU CAN COOK!

Barbecuing is a primal technique for cooking food; there is often nothing simpler. You don't always need fancy gadgets, just food and fire. By cooking directly in the embers of a fire, you take the simplest of foods and turn them into something special. You only need good embers, quality lumpwood charcoal, or the embers of a hardwood or fruitwood fire. You can then simply place the food straight in the embers... That's it. Here, I look at the simplest of barbecue techniques that use a minimal amount of kit, meaning anyone can achieve delicious results.

I love cooking in this way and I am massively inspired by proponents of this style, such as chefs Francis Mallmann, Adam Perry Lang, and Niklas Ekstedt. For certain ingredients there is no better way of cooking them—the exposure to direct heat caramelizes food like no other way. It is also a way of life—to appreciate food cooked outdoors, to experience lots of big bold flavors, to use your hands to eat, and to enjoy life to the full.

I grew up in front of the fire. On cold nights, my large family would sit in front of the flames and together we would cook honest, simple food in the embers of the fire. Jacket potatoes with charred crisp skin were the family favorite, a slab of butter melting into the middle. Toasting chestnuts in the embers was another prized activity and these taste memories are locked into my soul now. I then started to work in many far-flung places, where I was exposed to different flavors and new food cultures. I traveled extensively and learned to cook many new styles, constantly expanding my flavor palate. Visits to Morocco, Thailand, India, and Africa were all a huge influence on me.

When I moved to a house in rural Devon, south-west England, I started to cook more and more in the garden: campfires, smokers, and wood-fired ovens

all started to appear. This has built to an all-encompassing passion that is unbelievably versatile. On the one hand I cater for 12-course feasts, cooking over fire and smoke and serving my creations on long, elegantly dressed tables. On the other, I love to delve into the world of street food, dishing up humble but exciting creations inspired by grilling cultures around the world. One of my proudest moments was being crowned King of Meatopia at the inaugural London Meatopia, one of the UK's biggest barbecue events. You'll find my winning recipe for a *Dirty Tomahawk Steak* on page 27.

I love to show people what is possible with flame—from basic fire control to creating feasts—and explain how to cook on anything from simple fire pits to hi-tech pellet grills. This has led me to run a busy Facebook Group—CountryWoodSmoke—where people learn and share various artisanal techniques, such as bacon curing, smoking, and bread making. Alongside this I run the UK BBQ School, where I teach everyone from beginners to chefs looking to learn new skills. I also regularly host and demonstrate at outdoor cooking events, with whole weekends spent teaching butchery, fire control, grilling, smoking, and barbecuing. On top of that, I'm a barbecue judge at popular events including Grillstock, Qfest, and Pengrillie, and I am a Kansas City BBQ Society Certified BBQ Judge. You could say my passion for food and fire is all-encompassing.

For me, now, all of the best times spent with family and friends are in front of a fire, be it drinking whisky round the firepit with good mates, or sitting in front of the woodstove with my children, toasting marshmallows and chestnuts. I look forward to sharing some of these moments and the passion I have for food and fire with you.

TECHNIQUES

The life of a fire

This may sound rather deep for this book, but I'm a great believer in viewing a fire as you would a person's life. You have the inception, or the spark of fire that starts things off, the noisy crackle of an infant flame, and the youthful exuberance of a raging inferno. Things then calm down and you reach a plateau (which is the best time to cook), before settling into a comfortable, stable bed of embers and gradually dwindling away to ashes.

I see every time I light a fire as a huge opportunity to cook some wonderful food. If you make good use of the different stages of a fire's life, then you can maximize those opportunities to turn out memorable meals. For example, do you need the high searing heat of peak red-hot embers or a more sedate cinder bed for slow mellow cooking?

A fire is a simple thing of three parts:
Fuel – Air – Heat

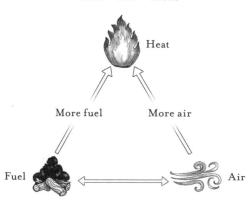

If you remove one of these parts, the fire will go out. However, if you understand how these parts relate to each other, then you will be able to control the heat on a barbecue. The most important part of a fire to maintain is what I call the "heart"—always have a portion of the fire where there is new fuel and a pile of embers to maintain the heat of the fire's heart. As soon as you spread out the embers, you lose the heart of the fire. You can always draw the embers out from the heart of the fire and cook over these. If you think a fire is cooling prematurely, then it may have lost its heart, so pull together some of the embers to create more heat and add more fuel.

A lot of people choose a gas barbecue because it's quick and the heat can be controlled easily by turning the dials. I see the control of heat on a wood or charcoal barbecue in a similar way. The first stage in managing a fire is controlling the amount of fuel you light; this is your primary temperature control. If you have too much lit fuel, then you will have a raging-hot fire (although this may be what you want, of course). Once you have a good feel for the amount of lit fuel that will provide different temperatures, you can tweak these temperatures using the air vents on the barbecue.

An air inlet on the base of most charcoal barbecues lets in air, while a vent on the top lets out heat and exhaust gases from the fire. I like to have the vent on the top just about fully open and  then I control the air getting to the coals with the air inlet. In a closed, airtight barbecue, the air going in must equal the air going out. It is very much like driving a car: I see the bottom inlet as the accelerator (the more open it is, the hotter the coals get) and the top vent as the brakes—if you close this vent down, the exhaust gases build up in the barbecue and cause the coals to cool down. When I'm driving a car, my preference is to control the speed by using more or less gas, rather than tapping the brakes. There are other ways to control the heat of a barbecue and hit certain temperatures, but these are my preferred techniques.

I advise you to get a feel for your own barbecue equipment, and the amount of fuel and air-inlet settings that will give a specific temperature zone. Try not to adjust the vents all the time... just relax, take your time, and the temperature will probably settle anyway. You'll find that you come into a special kind of relaxed state when you're in charge of your fire.

Setting up the coals in a kettle barbecue

I think a 22-inch (57cm) kettle barbecue is just about the best place to start as a barbecue novice, as it will provide you with a good opportunity to learn your fire-control techniques. Below are some charcoal configurations for cooking on a barbecue. Please note: none of these involves covering the entire base of the barbecue with charcoal. There is always a safe zone with no charcoal underneath the grill. That way, when the fat starts to render out of the food and drip onto the charcoal, you have somewhere to move the food so it doesn't flare up. This area is the indirect cooking zone.

Two-zone cooking
Set up around one-third to a half of the cooking area with hot coals underneath, so you have a direct zone (above the coals) and an indirect zone with no coals underneath. When you cook with a lid (which you should if you have one for your barbecue), the indirect zone is a wonderful place where you can cook larger pieces of food with less danger of burning them. When beginners are shown this technique in my barbecue classes, it can be a bit of a mind-blowing revelation for many. Banking the coals up to one side can give you even more space for indirect cooking. Some recipes, such as the *Barbecue Peach and Pork Balls* on page 96, require a little direct heat to sear the food first before being cooked/smoked in the indirect zone with the lid on.

"The snake"
This charcoal configuration is for the long, low, 'n' slow style of cooking. If you set up the snake correctly, it will hold a temperature of around 230–250°F (110–120°C) in the barbecue smoke zone for many hours, to allow for the slow smoking of ribs, pork butts, and even brisket. Bear in mind that you may need to add a few more coals to keep the fire going to cook a full brisket.

Down the middle
This is a great way to get a nice even cook without worrying too much about turning the food halfway through the cooking time. It's a great setup, but you need to make sure the coals contain enough heat to keep a good heart. You can get special baskets that hold the charcoal together and keep it burning nicely to maintain heat.

Lighting the fire

There are myriad ways you can start a barbecue fire, and I truly believe that how you start the fire sets the tone for the whole fire to come. Please avoid unnatural starters, such as paraffin cubes and lighter fluid, and certainly never use petrol. Products such as these will taint any fire and the food you cook in that fire. I think remnants of these remain long into a fire's life. Instead, buy a natural firelighter, which is great, and use some kindling to build up the fire. A chimney starter is a great way to get the coals going very quickly—you can be cooking within 10 minutes. A nice little cheat if you have electricity near your barbecue is to use an electric charcoal starter. This definitely feels like cheating, but you can have a charcoal barbecue or wood-fired oven roaring hot in a minute or two.

Going up through the gears

There will be lots of smoke at first, until the fire hits a critical point where the heat combusts the gases (i.e. the smoke) coming off the fuel. You will have a great deal of white smoke at this stage. This is dirty smoke. It is produced because the fire isn't hot enough and therefore not good to cook with. Once the fire hits a certain temperature, the smoke combusts and you have flame and a clean, thin, blue smoke. This is what you are aiming for. Usually, it's better to have a smaller, hotter fire with less smoke than a fire made with plenty of wood that you are trying to hold back, which creates more white smoke. You need air to take the fire up quickly through the heat gears toward the point where embers are forming and the fire can be more or less self-sustaining for a while—try a good few puffs from a pair of strong lungs, a fan, or an electric air blower (hairdryers are always popular). This will get your fire raging hot within minutes.

Move closer

Another way of controlling the temperature of a cook, which is frequently overlooked, is actually the simplest one. Barbecuers often only think of direct or indirect heat, but there is a wonderful middle road where the fire can "see" the food (even though it is still indirect heat). You achieve this heat by moving the food closer to the coals, which increases the cooking temperature, and moving it farther from the coals to reduce the temperature. Heat often travels in paths and eddies, but will mainly follow the easiest route of escape, so bear in mind where the vent for your barbecue is on the lid, as this can ramp up the temperatures underneath the vent more to the sides.

Temperature control

Temperature control is key when you are trying to elevate your cooking from good to great. Here are some points to consider.

Estimating the cooking temperature

The quickest way to estimate the cooking temperature is to put your hand very carefully around 6 inches (15cm)—conveniently, the height of a soft drinks can—above the cooking surface. The longer you can hold your hand there, the cooler the cooking temperature. This works for grills, wood-fired ovens, and firepits. Note: Please do this very carefully—I don't want you burning yourself and getting me into trouble… Here are the number of seconds you will be able to hold your hand above the cooking surface and the approximate temperatures to which these times equate:

Red hot	Less than 2 seconds/ instantaneous	660°F (350°C) +
High	2–3 seconds	530–660°F (280–350°C)
Medium hot	4–5 seconds	350–450°F (180–230°C)
Moderate	6–8 seconds	300–350°F (150–180°C)
Low to moderate	9–10 seconds	250–300°F (120–150°C)
Low	11–14 seconds	150–250°F (65–120°C)

I don't get too stressed about what temperature I'm cooking at, preferring to think of outdoor cooking in terms of temperature zones instead, as follows:

+ *Hot smoking*
(140–212°F/60–100°C)
You're looking for a slow smoke to cook food gently, so the fat doesn't start rendering; this is ideal for fish, such as hot-smoked salmon.

+ *Indirect barbecue smoking*
(212–265°F/100–130-ish°C)
You want the meat to smoke slowly for a long time, but the fats and collagen to render.

+ *Smoke roasting*
(320–400°F/160–200°C)
You want the food to crisp up and brown without charring. This is the golden zone where golden crispy chicken skin develops, for example.

+ *Searing*
(400–660°F/200–350°C)
This is the temperature at which you want to cook your steaks to get a nice seared crust.

+ *Red hot*
(660°F+/350°C+)
This is where you'd cook your pizzas.

Getting a more precise cooking temperature

Using a digital ambient thermometer that you leave in the barbecue is great for getting a more precise reading for the cooking temperature. Please don't rely on analog lid thermometers because they can be wildly inaccurate and are only useful as a rough guide.

Cooking to an internal temperature

As well as the cooking temperature for your barbecue, wood-fired oven, or smoker, and so on, there is also a specific internal temperature or temperature range you need to achieve for various meats and fish (see the *Internal Temperature Guide,* on page 13). There are three main methods for working out when food is cooked to your desired internal temperature:

USING TIME: This is the least accurate method to use because there are so many variables, including the starting temperature of the meat, the temperature of the barbecue, and the thickness, fat content, and water content of the food you're cooking. When cooking to a recipe, time should only ever be a rough guide.

USING TEMPERATURE: Cooking to a specific internal temperature is the biggest step forward that anyone who barbecues can take. By using a digital probe thermometer, you are ensuring your food is cooked sufficiently and is safe to eat. Cooking to temperature will be a huge boost to your confidence. As well as feeling confident that your food is safe to eat, you will also know that it is cooked as you like it. With so many variables, this is my preferred choice and what I teach in my barbecue school classes in the UK.

USING TOUCH: I'm not a huge fan of estimating a steak's temperature by touch because every piece of steak feels different as it cooks, depending on the way it has been cut and how strong the muscle fibers are. If you are very experienced, then fine, but most beginners struggle with this. Where feel becomes really important is with slow-smoked cuts, such as pork butts, pork and beef ribs, and especially brisket.

Although cooking to an internal temperature will probably get you about right in terms of the collagens in the meat breaking down, you'll also need to go by feel to get the cook spot on. As meat comes into contact with heat, the collagens tense up, especially when you get past a temperature of 140–160°F (60–70°C). To get the collagens to relax and break down, you need to take the temperature of the meat above 194°F (90°C). In this zone, each piece of meat will have an exact temperature when it's ready—a digital probe thermometer will go through meat like warm butter at this point. This temperature might be in the high 170s°F (80s°C) or even up to 207–208°F (97–98°C), and is dependent on many factors. So, cooking something like brisket is the ultimate test of the barbecuer's skill, as waiting until it's ready is a true test of patience. In fact, many briskets are taken off the smoker too early and end up being tough. I teach my students how meat feels when it is ready at my Intermediate Barbecue class, as I think this is something that you can only properly understand if you have felt it for yourself—and it will stay with you forever.

Staying Safe

Whenever you're cooking with live fire, remember that any nearby surfaces will get hot, sparks can fly, and hot liquid and fat may spill onto your skin. Always have a first-aid kit, as well as a fire extinguisher and fire blanket, close to where you are cooking. And always supervise children near a barbecue or fire.

Internal Temperature Guide

A key aspect of this book is cooking to a specific internal temperature or temperature range, which is provided with each recipe. In some of the recipes, I have made suggestions for what I consider to be the best internal cooking temperature, but feel free to adjust this for meats such as beef and lamb that can be cooked to suit personal taste. Be especially careful to cook poultry and pork products to the stated temperature to destroy harmful germs and ensure the meat is properly cooked through.

• BEEF/ LAMB / VEAL / VENISON

Blue	115–120°F (46–49°C)
Rare	125–130°F (52–55°C)
Medium rare	130–140°F (55–60°C)
Medium	140–150°F (60–65°C)
Medium well	150–155°F (65–69°C)
Well done	160–212°F (71–100°C)

• PORK

Medium	145°F (63°C)
Well done	160°F (71°C)

• POULTRY

N/A	165°F (74°C)

• FISH

N/A	145°F (63°C)

Sourcing meats

I prefer to buy my meat from a good local butcher. I am lucky that I can buy meat from local farm stores as well as direct from the farmer. I suggest you find a place that can supply you with meat of a quality you're happy with. Try to build a good rapport with your meat suppliers, as they should be able to help you find some of the more unusual cuts that barbecuers are fond of.

Storing Dry Rubs, Bastes, and Sauces

Using dry rubs, bastes, and sauces will take your barbecue cooking to the next level. Always keep dry rubs in airtight containers out of direct sunlight in a cool, dry place, to ensure they last as long as possible. Any wet bastes or sauces can be kept for a short time in the refrigerator.

Cleaning the barbecue

I advise you to clean a barbecue while it is still warm. I prefer to use a scrunched-up ball of heavy-duty foil on the grill surface to keep it clean. Be careful of using barbecue-cleaning products on the inside, as the smells can linger and taint the food. You can also use a good blast of heat to clean up a barbecue nicely as well, so run your barbecue really hot every now and again—this is also a good time to cook a steak.

EQUIPMENT AND MATERIALS

Barbecues

First things first, I guess having some sort of barbecue is pretty useful. You can cook wonderful meals on a cheap grill over a circle of stones for most foods that require grilling, but it will be harder to regulate temperatures for slower cooking or larger bits of meat using this setup until you have become more experienced in fire and heat management. Personally, I enjoy cooking in a simple hearth with a Tuscan grill over the coals. This is a simple, square, solid cast-iron grill on legs that you pop over a bed of embers—it's simple, but does a great job. Mine is so well used that it has a real character of its own; I lost one of the legs at some point, but it still stands sturdy over the embers.

However, for most people, a large 22-inch (57-cm), good-quality kettle barbecue is the best place to start, and a good-quality one of these will see you through many years. A large kettle barbecue also has enough space to allow for indirect cooking with the lid on. A slightly different option—if you're planning on doing more smoking and less grilling—would be a bullet smoker. This gives you many options for cooking, plus plenty of space for food, but is less useful if you plan to do lots of grilling.

Popular types of barbecue

Once you have mastered heat control, there are many choices of barbecue, as follows:

22-INCH (57-CM) KETTLE BARBECUE: Easy to learn on, with lots of space for indirect cooking. However, the coals don't last too long and will probably need topping up every few hours.

GAS GRILL: Quick and easy to turn on and get hot for cooking. This type of barbecue never gets as hot as

good charcoal and food cooked on one can sometimes lack flavor.

OFFSET SMOKER: Gives an authentic barbecue flavor and there's room for plenty of food. This smoker needs barbecue "baby-sitting" and constant tending. It can also be tricky to run with unstable temperatures.

PELLET GRILL: So easy and efficient—just turn it on and forget about it. There are lower levels of smoke for some; it perhaps makes the craft of barbecue too easy.

BULLET SMOKERS: Great for learning how to smoke food, this is reliable and produces good results. However, there is not a huge amount of room for lots of food.

PORTABLE CHARCOAL GRILL: There are plenty of awesome options in this category these days, and some great grills available from Japan, Germany, India, and the Philippines. A portable grill allows you to grill small pieces of food and can be taken on the road with you.

Essential equipment

Very few tools are essential for cooking outdoors. After all, our ancestors managed to cook meat on a campfire very successfully, and I sometimes like to go back to this "naked" style of cooking, relying on my senses to know when the food is cooked correctly and how hot the fuel is burning. Barbecuing is easier if you have the following items (the most important of which is probably a good knife):

Good knife

Having a good knife to work with is important and very much a personal choice. So I recommend you try out a range of knives, picking them up and seeing what feels good in your hands.

Digital probe thermometer

The first piece of barbecue equipment I encourage people to buy is a digital probe thermometer, which is used to measure the internal temperature of the food. There are lots of brands available, but most serious barbecuers have a Thermapen on their person at pretty much all times because they are reliable, accurate, and very fast at reading the temperature.

Charcoal chimney charter

The second bit of kit I suggest you buy is a charcoal chimney starter. Although there are other quicker ways to light a fire, this is quick, reliable, and effective, and you can leave it heating up while you are preparing the food (or drinking beer).

Pair of tongs

The final essential is a good pair of sturdy tongs, as you'll need to pick up and move food around a hot grill or smoker. Not only should the tongs be sturdy enough to handle a large chunk of meat, but also feel good in your hands. There is a wide range of tongs available, so try a few out and see which pair works best for you.

And for the cook

Oh, yes, and a nice cold drink... you always need a nice cold drink to keep you hydrated when cooking.

Kit to make life easier

In addition to the essential kit, there are other pieces of equipment that you'll find useful, as well as beneficial if you are looking to improve your barbecuing skills.

Digital ambient thermometer

As well as a digital probe thermometer that shows you the internal temperature of the food, it's also helpful to have a digital ambient thermometer, which reads the temperature of the barbecue or smoker when the lid is down. It's very important to have one of these, especially when you're learning the art of heat control. It shows the effect that any changes you make are having on the temperature you are cooking at. You can also use the thermometer to monitor the temperature without lifting the lid too often, and that's a good thing. The analog thermometers that you get on most barbecues are pretty unreliable and inaccurate, and catch a lot of beginners out.

Electric blower

If you light a lot of fires, then having some sort of electric blower will save a lot of puff. I mostly use an electric looftlighter these days. This powerful combined heater and blower will get your coals or fire lit in a couple of minutes. It's probably cheating... but hey.

Cast-iron skillets or pans

These nearly made the list of essential equipment. Although not crucial, they are pretty important if you want to cook with sauces or ingredients that will go too soft on a grill. They're also vital for cooking in a wood-fired oven. A range of sizes is useful, with handles that can take the heat of a barbecue or wood-fired oven.

Nice to have

This is the, oh boy where do I start list. A few years ago, here in the UK, we were very limited in terms of the toys we could get for our barbecue endeavors, but with the huge growth of outdoor cooking, the market for cool toys and gadgets has taken off. Now there are Wi-Fi-enabled smoker controllers, giving you a good night's sleep, and all sorts of Bluetooth gadgets that make monitoring your cook easy. These are all great—I love toys as much as the next person. The barbecue kit that's available varies hugely, depending on what your style of cooking is, so think carefully about what will make your life easier.

A rotisserie is another nice bit of kit for the keen barbecuer, although it can be expensive. If you decide to invest in one, ensure it is robust. Battery-operated rotisseries will probably be able to handle a chicken or small roasting joint, but a house-current (mains-powered) version is necessary for larger meats and a few chickens. Use stainless-steel spits and prongs, as these won't rust. You'll also need some sort of stand if you're cooking over an open fire. All sorts of wonderful accessories, such as baskets and rotating kebab skewers, can be added to a rotisserie.

Wood-fired cooking kit

When cooking with wood as the main fuel source, you'll need some different bits of kit, one of the most important of which is a pair of welder's gauntlets for handling pots and other hot items. A peel for pizzas and moving pans around is also vital. A favorite tool is a 3-foot (90-cm) long piece of copper pipe with the ends rounded off and flattened. You can use this to give a quick puff of air to a fire that's lost its heat—just remember to blow only and never suck.

Another very useful tool to have when cooking with a wood-fired oven is an infrared pistol thermometer, which gives a good accurate temperature for the base or roof of a wood-fired oven.

If you have a wood-fired oven, a good, sharp hand axe and a solid chopping log are definitely required, for chopping bits of kindling and splitting down large logs.

Cooking location and environment

Where you choose to cook has a huge effect on the performance of your barbecue. For example, an exposed and windy location can cool your barbecue down significantly. So choose somewhere that is relatively sheltered, but be wary of neighbors who might not welcome your smoky activities (the best way to overcome this is to invite them round for a meal).

The biggest factor in ensuring that I can enjoy barbecues outdoors all year round is having a simple roof over my outdoor kitchen. We were getting pretty fed up of weather-watching, and canceling parties and barbecues, so decided that a simple roof would make a huge difference, and we were right. Many people now build little outdoor cooking shacks. Some are simple affairs, using pop-up gazebos, while others are more fancy and have a proper roof and built-in kitchen units. You'll find that even a simple lean-to roof will make outdoor cooking a much more pleasurable experience.

Fuels

I've always looked at the fuel I use as a critical ingredient in my outdoor cooking. The charcoal or wood that you choose will have a huge bearing on the quality of heat and smoke that your fire produces. This effect is very much understood by those who cook regularly with fire. Once you have tried a really good charcoal, there is no going back to the stuff you get from a service station (garage) again…

Charcoal

As with the meat you choose, the charcoal you use on your barbecue will be down to a price versus quality relationship—we all have a price that we can afford, especially when we cook outdoors a lot. So, go for the best-quality charcoal you can afford. Factors that determine quality include how well the charcoal is cooked, the wood it's made from, and its sustainability. Needless to say, using poor-quality charcoal will give you a poor end result; cheaper charcoals can have off-flavors and be overly smoky. I've found bits of rubber, rope, and brick in some charcoal I've used, and these obviously affect the food. Also, please don't use instant-light charcoal, which contains waxy propellants so the charcoal lights quickly, but will taint your food. There are a few types of charcoal to choose from:

LUMP CHARCOAL: A good-quality lump charcoal will make your barbecue experience, and the quality of the food you cook, much better. It's quick to light and burns well—depending on the variety of wood used, it can burn for a long time, too. If you're using the "dirty" (i.e. on the embers) technique, then this is the charcoal you should use.

BRIQUETTES: The quality of briquettes varies considerably. A cheap briquette is loaded with fillers and binding agent. But there are also good-quality briquettes available, so make sure to use those. Briquettes have a long and steady burn, and go very ashy.

COCOSHELL: This is a wonderful environmentally friendly by-product of the coconut industry, and is made from the carbonized shells of coconuts. The cocoshell comes in cubes, briquettes, and extruded logs. It burns clean and gives off a good consistent heat.

Wood

When using wood as the main fuel source, you need to bear a few things in mind, including how you want to cook, the heat level you want to use, the amount of embers you need, and the smoke. Cooking in the open, perhaps on a campfire or with an asado setup (using only fire and a grill), the smoke has less of an effect, but the heat output and embering up are the most important of these. Cooking in a wood-fired oven definitely needs a high heat-producing wood, such as silver birch. The nice thing is that you can mix up different types of wood—for example, a mix of silver birch for heat and oak for embers is a great combination for a campfire. The oak alone will probably just smolder and smoke, but the silver birch will give a bit of heat and smoke less.

THE MORE SMOKE, THE BETTER?: Well, actually, no... When I first started barbecue'ing and smoking many years ago, I would use too much wood and the food was always very smoky. I learnt quite quickly that this isn't a good thing—if all you can taste is a strong smoke, this is akin to licking out an ashtray. As my outdoor cooking has improved, I've noticed that I'm using less and less smoke, and looking for more of a balanced harmony of flavors. Smoke is a seasoning, just like salt and pepper, and once overdone, you can't go back. Please note: the taste of smoke on food will be stronger when it is contained (i.e. if you are cooking with a lid)

DUST, CHIPS, CHUNKS, OR LOGS: The size of the pieces of wood you use on a barbecue will affect the smoke level of the food—for example, finer dusts tend to burn out very quickly, so are best reserved for cold smoking. Wood chips are best used for short cooks, where you want to impart a good smoke in a short space of time, perhaps for something like chicken or fish. Chunks are my go-to size for placing on charcoal for a bit of smoke—I use one or two golf-ball-sized chunks for most smoking, to give a lovely gentle smoke. Some people like things a bit smokier, and that's okay, so simply use more. But remember that standing in close proximity to a smoker for a while will desensitize you to the smoke, so what might be nicely smoked for you could be a massively overpowering smoke for someone else. Logs are best reserved for open firepits and campfires, and offset burners. Go for well-seasoned logs, as kiln-dried wood can be too dry (although this is my choice for wood-fired oven cooking).

TYPES OF WOOD: Lots of types of wood can be used for cooking outdoors, and most people will have their favorites. I urge you to experiment, and try out the woods available in your area. See what kind of smoke they produce, the amount of heat they give off, and how well they ember up. Here are a few guidelines to bear in mind when cooking with wood:

+   Only use hardwood, fruitwood, and nutwood (softwoods such as pine aren't generally suitable for cooking)

+   Don't use treated woods

+   Don't use painted woods

    NOTE: If you're unsure of the type of wood, then don't use it.

MY FAVORITE UK WOODS ARE:

+   **Silver birch**: My favorite, with a lovely smoke, lots of heat, and short-lived embers

+   **English oak**: Good for moderate heat, but has a tendency to smolder; provides long-lived embers; and produces a strong smoke that's easy to overdo

+   **Ash**: Great heat; moderately long-lived embers; and a gentle smoke

+   **Cherry**: My second favorite wood, with a lovely sweet smoke; embers that last well; and gives food a lovely color

+   **Beech**: Similar to birch, but the smoke is more subtle, and the embers last well

+   **Apple**: Lovely, fragrant, sweet smoke; burns well; and the embers last well

+   **Pear**: Similar to apple, but with a more subtle, cleaner smoke

WOODS TO USE FROM OVERSEAS (I.E. FROM THE USA):

+   **Hickory**: Wonderful wood for smoking; food that is hickory-smoked smells of bacon

+   **Pecan**: Gentler version of oak, with a lovely smoke

+   **American oak**: Wonderful, complex smoke with toast, vanilla, and a touch of spice

There are plenty of recommended woods for each type of food, but please experiment and find out what works best for you. Please remember to use a subtle smoke for delicate foods such as seafood and save stronger-smoking woods for food that can handle it.

You can, of course, also combine different types of woods when smoking. For example, you can add cherry to anything—a few of my favorite combinations are cherry and hickory for chicken and pork, or cherry and pecan/oak for beef.

Other things to add smoke

Woody herbs, such as thyme, rosemary, and bay, are great for adding a perfumed hit of smoke to food, but be careful, as the smoke from these is very fragrant and strong. This means they can easily overpower the food you are cooking when contained in a barbecue or smoker with a lid. I prefer to use these gently in an open-fire situation, in a firepit or fire bowl, campfire, or hearth setup.

Dry Rubs

A dry rub is a wonderful thing in the world of barbecue, and can be either incredibly simple or hugely complex. A dry rub works with the food on which it is sprinkled. I'm always wary of using too much dry rub as it can overpower the food—a gentle and even sprinkling is my preferred way of preparing food with a dry rub. Using a set of digital scales to weigh the ingredients in grams for the dry rubs will give you more accurate measurements.

For the 50/50 Rub:
Equal parts sea salt and freshly
  ground black pepper

For the All-purpose Rub:
2¼ tbsp (30g) packed (soft)
  light brown sugar
1⅓ tbsp (20g) fine sea salt
2 tsp (7g) garlic granules
2 tsp (4g) smoked paprika
1 tsp (3g) freshly ground black
  pepper
½ tsp (2g) chipotle powder

For the Coffee Rub:
2 tbsp (30g) fine sea salt
1½ tbsp (20g) packed (soft)
  light brown or turbinado
  (demerara) sugar
2⅓ tbsp (20g) freshly cracked
  black pepper
1¼ tsp (5g) garlic granules
2g ground coffee

50/50 Rub

This is a great rub for beef. Whenever I am cooking a roast beef joint on
the barbecue, this is what I normally use. It's great on chuck, short ribs,
brisket, and so on. Add some garlic granules if you want to mix things
up a little.

All-purpose Rub

This is a simple, well-balanced dry rub that suits most things, especially
chicken and pork. You can add plenty of other ingredients, such as
dried herbs or some extra chili powder and other spices, to the basic
rub, or take it in pretty much any direction you choose. Regard the
all-purpose rub as a good base on which to build and come up with your
own variations. The recipe (left) has a gentle smokiness from the
paprika and chipotle, and a little heat.

Coffee Rub

A basic coffee-based rub is great to have in your barbecue repertoire.
It works well on a lot of cuts of beef, but also surprisingly well on pork
chops. The coffee gives a nice depth of flavor to the rub. Again, regard
this as a base recipe—if you wish, simply add other ingredients, such as
spices like ground cumin and extra chili powder, for a bit of a kick, and
take the rub in a new direction.

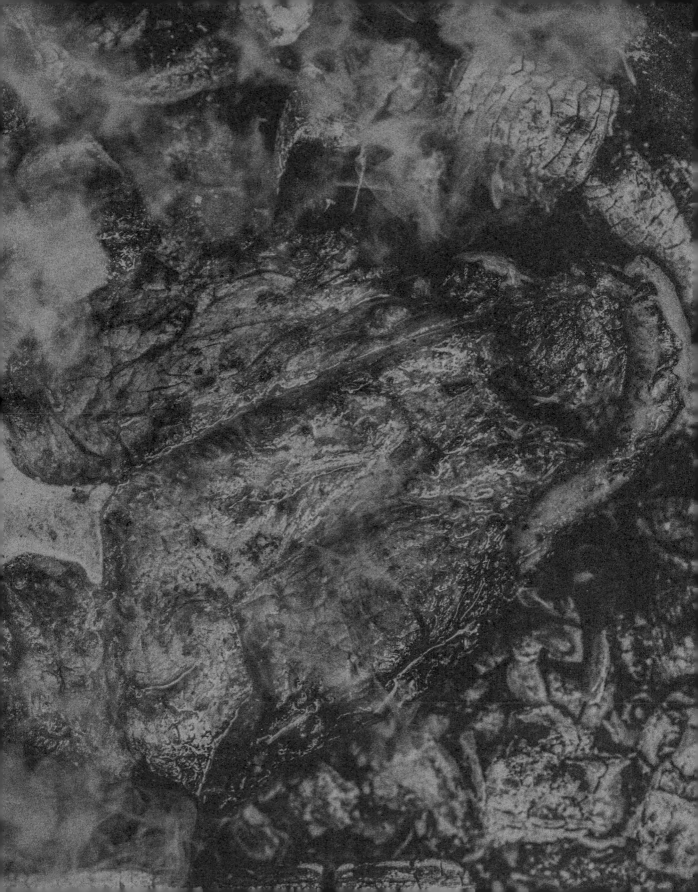

1

DIRTY

There's something truly elemental about putting food straight onto the embers of a burning fire, often called "Dirty" or Caveman style. The food takes on the spirit of the wood or charcoal that is burning, so you need to use the best-quality hardwood or charcoal you can— no briquettes, gas-station-bought charcoal, or instant light here. Equipment-wise, you need very little: a few bricks or stones to contain the embers or a small grill. Get the embers good and hot, either by burning down a hardwood fire to embers, or by getting some top-quality lump charcoal burning until it's screaming hot. Many people use hairdryers or blowers, or simply their own puff to get the coals hot; there is then very little ash on the surface. Afterward, you simply leave the food on the coals—no fiddling—and allow a beautiful seared crust to form. You can also harness the power of charcoal to melt fats onto resting food, either by using a lump of red-hot charcoal or with the searing heat of a flambadou.

Dirty Ribeye Roast

RECOMMENDED HEAT:
Red-hot lump charcoal.

SERVES 8

9lb (4kg) ribeye roast joint

For the Dirty baste:

Generous sprig each of
fresh thyme, rosemary,
and flat-leaf parsley

2 garlic cloves

2 tbsp coarse sea salt

Good few glugs of olive oil

1 tsp lemon juice

1 canned anchovy fillet

To serve:

Salad

Bold red wine (optional)

Cooking "dirty" does not have to be limited to small bits of steak or other quickly cooked pieces of food. As with all the techniques in this book, you can mix and match the methods. For example, if you want to slow-smoke a big chunk of beef, such as this beautiful ribeye roast joint, and then finish off with a dirty sear (that is, a reverse dirty), or sear dirty on the coals first before smoking up to medium rare, just go for it. This large ribeye roast joint was dry-aged for 40 days and purchased from a butcher in Aberdeen, Scotland.

Remove the meat from the refrigerator a couple of hours prior to cooking and let come to room temperature.

To make my Dirty baste, blitz the fresh herbs, garlic, sea salt, olive oil, lemon juice, and anchovy fillet in a food processor or using a hand blender.

Pop the whole joint straight onto some lump charcoal and cook for a few minutes on each side until it crusts up perfectly on the outside.

Place the joint on the grate indirectly away from the coals, at 300°F (150°C), and brush generously all over with the baste.

Smoke the joint indirectly with the barbecue lid down until the internal temperature of the beef reaches 115–120°F (46–49°C) for rare and around 130–140°F (55–60°C) for medium rare.

Here, the roast was pulled at 115°F (46°C) and allowed to rest until the temperature reached 116°F (47°C).

+

GRILL TIPS

There are so many ways to cook on a barbecue, so I suggest seeing what works best for you. A lot of barbecuing is trial and error, and mixing up wonderful, live fire–cooking techniques— in this case, smoking and dirty searing. Be bold, be confident, and have fun.

Dirty Steak with Melted Bone Marrow

RECOMMENDED HEAT:
Level bed of red-hot embers using best-quality lump charcoal or the embers of a hardwood fire (with silver birch, for example).

SERVES 1

1 steak

Coarse sea salt and freshly ground black pepper

For the melted bone marrow:

4 tbsp bone marrow

1 garlic clove, finely chopped

Sprig of fresh rosemary, finely chopped

Sprig of fresh thyme, finely chopped

2 sprigs of fresh flat-leaf parsley, finely chopped

I've enjoyed cooking "dirty" steaks for many years now. I started doing them in my wood-fired oven on some embers, as I didn't have a grilling grate that would fit through the door of the oven. So I just raked forward the embers and cooked the steaks on these. I didn't realize then that this technique was something others were doing, but I've since seen many other masters of this method. These days, I tend to cook my dirty steaks on top-quality charcoal in a grill, but still enjoy cooking them on the embers of a silver-birch fire when I can. This recipe is another in my series of experiments in resting meats and then adding an extra layer of flavors during the resting period. I love bone marrow—they call it "God's Butter" for very good reason. It's rich, fatty, and delicious, and perfect for basting. If you can get bone marrow from good-quality, dry-aged beef, then you have something very special.

Prepare the bone marrow in advance by mixing it with the garlic and finely chopped herbs. Wrap in foil or plastic wrap (clingfilm), form into a rough sausage shape, and pop in the refrigerator to firm up for a few hours.

Put the steak on the embers. Don't season the steak with salt until the last minute—instead, wait until you flip the meat over before seasoning with sea salt and black pepper to taste. Putting on salt too early draws moisture to the surface of the meat, which will boil off and give you a gray steak and a poor sear. To get the best sear, season the steak after flipping. Only flip the steak once, and don't move, fiddle with, or press down on it in between.

+
GRILL TIPS

You can use any type of steak, but my favorites for this particular cooking method are hanger, skirt, sirloin, and bone-in ribeye.

Use a digital probe thermometer to check when the steak is a few degrees off your desired cooking temperature, depending on how you like your steak (see *Internal Temperature Guide*, page 13), then remove from the coals and let rest for a moment.

Remove the bone marrow from the fridge and cut off a thick slice. Place the slice of bone marrow on top of the steak, then pop a piece of red-hot charcoal or flaming silver-birch kindling on top to melt the marrow onto the steak.

Dirty Tomahawk Steak

RECOMMENDED HEAT:
Use good-quality lump charcoal and get the coals nice and hot in the grill. Wait for the flames to die down before cooking the steaks.

SERVES 2–4

2 tomahawk steaks, each about 32oz (900g)

For the baste:

2 garlic cloves

3 sprigs each of fresh rosemary, thyme, and flat-leaf parsley

3 tbsp coarse rock salt

6 tbsp olive oil

Squeeze of fresh lemon

To serve:

Green salad

Cooked vegetables of your choice

Cooked rice

Crusty sourdough

I always enjoy visiting my local butcher, especially when he has something a bit special to try. This time, it was some Aberdeen Angus tomahawk steaks that had been dry-aged for at least 50 days—I knew I had to taste them. These are essentially the ribeye steak "Côte de Boeuf" with the full rib bone trimmed and kept long. This is the pinnacle of big joints of dry-aged beef, which I like to cook straight on the coals, "dirty" style. It's so simple and I really urge you to give this method of cooking a go. The meat develops really deep flavors that will blow you away. Trust me, you will never look back.

First, make the baste by blitzing all the ingredients in a food processor or using a hand blender until you have a bright green paste.

Brush each steak with some baste and place each one straight on the coals. Cook for a few minutes on each side, basting every now and again. Place the steaks to one side of the grill to smoke with the barbecue lid down for 20 minutes until they reach the desired internal temperature of 115°F (46°C). Remove from the coals and rest for 10 minutes.

Cut the steaks into thin slices, and serve with a green salad, some cooked vegetables, cooked rice, and crusty sourdough.

+

GRILL TIPS

Dry-aging beef brings out the most amazing nutty, blue cheese tastes and renders the beef as tender as you can get. It's perfect served "bleu" with an internal temperature of 115°F (46°C), and with a salty herby crust on the outside. I really think it's difficult to top this way of cooking a good steak.

Pork Chops with Charcoal-melted Nduja Butter

RECOMMENDED HEAT:
Barbecue that allows both direct
and indirect cooking at 320–
350°F (160–180°C) with the lid
on. Add a small chunk of wood for
smoking (I use hickory, but cherry,
apple, and maple also work well).

SERVES 2

1 "double" two-bone pork chop

3 tbsp CountryWoodSmoke
  Mocha Rub (or a pork rub of
  your choice)

For the nduja butter:

2 tbsp soft unsalted butter

2 tbsp nduja

A good-quality pork chop is a thing of beauty, with creamy fat and a thick loin. However, even with the best pork, it's still a relatively blank canvas on which you can layer some seriously good flavor combinations. And that is the beauty of barbecue—there are so many opportunities to layer flavors and few things are better than when all those flavors work in joyous harmony. This recipe works these flavor-layering opportunities to the maximum. You have the meat base, the dry rub, the smoke and searing, and the final theatrical flourish: a slick of spicy, russet-colored nduja butter melted and seared with a piece of red-hot lump charcoal. Nduja is a soft, spreadable salami from Calabria, in Italy, that is mostly pork fat, but has plenty of chili for a real kick. If you haven't discovered the joy that is nduja, then you must try it, as it has so many wonderful uses.

Make the nduja butter in advance by combining the butter and nduja. This is a type of compound butter. Wrap in plastic wrap (clingfilm) or foil and roll into a sausage shape. Pop in the refrigerator or freezer until the butter has firmed up.

Score the fat on the pork chop or the rind if this is left on and you want some crackling.

Sprinkle the chop with an even coating of the dry rub and place directly over the charcoal with the fat-side facing down. Put on the lid and cook for a few minutes until the fat starts to render and crisp up—you'll know this is happening because the amount of white smoke from the top vent will increase as the fat drops onto the charcoal. Sear the chop on both sides until you get the sear you want.

Move the chop to the indirect area of the barbecue, and let cook slowly with the lid on until it reaches an internal temperature of 145°F (63°C). You can pull the chop a couple of degrees earlier, if you wish, as the temperature will continue to rise by a few degrees while the chop is resting.

Remove the chop from the barbecue and let rest for 5 minutes, then cut in half between the ribs and across the center.

Put a slice of nduja butter on the cut side of the chop, then quickly place a piece of red-hot lump charcoal from the barbecue on top of the butter. This will smoke and melt the butter onto the chop—the cut side of the pork will soak up the butter to add a wonderful extra depth of flavor.

Serve on a plate with the lump of sizzling charcoal on top for some great table theater, allowing the diner to remove the charcoal and get stuck in.

+

GRILL TIPS

If you can't get hold of nduja, try making a herby, garlicky compound butter or a nice blue cheese compound butter instead. Melting and searing flavored butter into the meat is a technique that takes the humble pork chop to a whole new level.

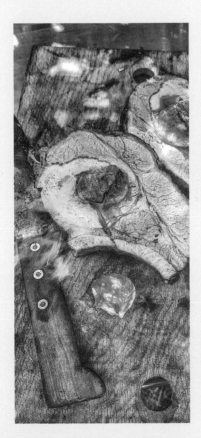

PORK CHOPS WITH CHARCOAL-MELTED NDUJA BUTTER

Scallops on a Silver-birch Log

A good, plump, sweet scallop is a sublime work of art that needs very little cooking—just a quick sear on both sides to keep it quivering and juicy. It requires a bold hand to place such a beautiful ingredient on a dirty lump of smoldering wood, but this is exactly what you'll need to do here… Trust me, it's good.

RECOMMENDED HEAT:
Split a silver-birch log, at least 1 inch (2.5cm) in diameter, in half down the middle to give you a flat side on which to cook the scallops. Fire up the barbecue with good-quality lump charcoal and place the log on top of the grill. Let burn for a good while, taking in the mouth-watering smoke of the silver birch as it heats up. Once the surface of the log is turning white and starting to get a little ash-y, you know it's time to cook.

SERVES 1

3 good-quality fresh scallops, roe (corals) attached

2 lemon slices

Coarse sea salt and freshly ground black pepper

To serve:

Large handful of arugula (rocket)

Give the log a quick blow to remove any loose ash, then place the scallops on the flat side of the wood. Season to taste with a little sea salt and add a couple of slices of lemon to caramelize.

After a few minutes, the edges of the scallops will start to crisp up, which means they are ready to turn. Flip the scallops over and give them a further 2–3 minutes. They should develop a delicate crust, but still be soft and juicy on the inside, having taken on a sweet smoky flavor.

Serve the scallops on a bed of arugula (rocket) with the caramelized lemon slices, and season to taste with a little more sea salt and some black pepper.

+

GRILL TIPS

Instead of using chimichurri, finish the scallops with some garlic and lemon butter or perhaps nduja butter (see page 28)—both these butters make a good alternative.

Scallops in the Shell with Sorrel Chimichurri

RECOMMENDED HEAT:
Good level bed of red-hot embers of good-quality lump charcoal or the embers of a hardwood fire.

SERVES 1

3 cleaned good-quality scallops in the shell, roe (corals) attached

For the sorrel chimichurri:

Handful of fresh flat-leaf parsley

1 cup (30g) fresh sorrel

6 garlic cloves

1 small shallot, chopped

4–5 tbsp red wine vinegar, to taste

3 tbsp cold water

2 tbsp extra-virgin olive oil

Juice of ½ lemon

1 tsp coarse sea salt

1 tsp dried oregano

1 tsp red pepper (dried chili) flakes

Cooking a scallop in its shell provides a natural "mini pan" to contain any juices that are released, or any sauces/butters you add. You can place the scallop shell directly on the charcoal to make the most of the searing heat of direct embers. You probably won't achieve the same seared crust as you would if cooking the scallop on a red-hot plancha or pan, but you get a lovely, juicy cooked scallop (and have no extra pan to wash up).

Chimichurri is mostly associated with beef in its native Argentina, but I find it complements a great number of grilled seafood dishes and vegetables with its punchy herbiness. If you want a delicately sauced dish, this probably isn't for you, but I love the way a little drizzle of chimichurri works with the sweetness of the scallops. The sorrel in the chimichurri gives a little added lemon zip to the dish. If you can't find sorrel in your local grocery store, try the herb section of a garden center.

Make the chimichurri in advance by blitzing all the ingredients in a food processor or using a hand blender until you have a coarse chunky paste. Add a little more olive oil, if required.

Ensure the scallops are free from their shells using a small sharp knife. Place each scallop in its shell on the embers. Let cook in the shell for a few minutes until you see the juices starting to brown—this is the time to turn the scallop over.

Before turning the scallops over (within their shells), drizzle each one with 1 teaspoon of the chimichurri—don't use too much or you will overpower the sweet scallop. Cook the scallops for a few more minutes, ensuring they do not burn, then serve.

Ember-cooked Figs

RECOMMENDED HEAT:
Good level bed of embers of best-quality lump charcoal or the embers of a hardwood fire. The embers need to be red-hot, so ensure there is enough airflow by cooking without a lid.

SERVES 1

2 ripe figs
To serve:
Salad leaves of your choice
3½oz (100g) feta cheese, crumbled
1 tsp runny honey

Figs have their own protective skin that makes them perfect for popping straight into the embers, "dirty" style. The skin crisps up and protects the sweet sticky center, the heat caramelizing the sugars to give a wonderfully complex, sweet caramel flavor. You can use the figs in any number of dishes, knowing you have made the best possible use of them. Here, I made a simple salad using the cooked figs, some salty feta cheese, and a drizzle of honey, along with a few salad leaves—something with a little heat or pepperiness works well.

Nestle the figs in the embers, pointed end facing up, and leave for 3–4 minutes. Turn the figs over and leave for a few more minutes, or until the skin is slightly charred and blistered. How do you know when the figs are ready? Well, they'll start to sing a sweet song... you'll hear them hissing slightly as the juice gets hot and starts to escape. You will also notice a wonderful caramel scent in the air as the sugars in the figs caramelize.

Remove the figs from the embers with a pair of tongs, and let cool slightly.

Cut the figs in half or into slices, and serve on a platter with the salad leaves, crumbled feta, and a drizzle of runny honey.

Ember-cooked Vegetables

RECOMMENDED HEAT:
Good level bed of embers of
best-quality lump charcoal in
a barbecue or the embers of a
hardwood fire (I like to use silver
birch). The embers need to be
red-hot, so ensure there is enough
airflow by cooking without a lid.

SERVES 2

2 ripe tomatoes

2 shallots, peeled

1 zucchini (courgette)

1 small eggplant (aubergine)

1 red, orange, and green bell
(sweet) pepper, cored and
deseeded, but left whole

For the chermoula:

2 large garlic cloves

1 red chili pepper

Handful of cilantro (fresh
coriander)

6 tbsp extra-virgin olive oil

2 tbsp white wine vinegar

Juice of 1 lemon

2 tsp paprika

2 tsp ground cumin

Pinch of sea salt

For the flatbreads:

1 cup (125g) all-purpose (plain)
flour, plus extra for dusting

5 tbsp (75ml) warm water

½ tbsp olive oil

½ tsp fine sea salt

Cooking vegetables in the embers of some good-quality lump charcoal or a hardwood fire really intensifies their flavor and adds a wonderful charred element to any dish they are added to. Here, I made some flatbreads to wrap the vegetables in and then added some zingy chermoula.

Make the chermoula in advance by blitzing all the ingredients in a food processor or using a hand blender until you have a loose paste. Add more olive oil, if required. Set aside.

To prepare the flatbreads, mix all the ingredients together in a bowl, either by hand or using a food mixer with a dough hook, until you have a smooth dough. Knead the dough for 8–10 minutes. Pop the dough in the bowl, cover with plastic wrap (clingfilm), and let rest for 20–30 minutes at room temperature.

Split the dough into four equal pieces. Dust your work surface with a little flour. Roll the pieces of dough into very thin rounds, or whichever shape you prefer, using a rolling pin.

Bake the flatbreads on the embers of the barbecue or hardwood fire for a few minutes on each side, or until just charred and crisped up in places. (You can, of course, also use a hot barbecue grill.) Set aside and wrap in a clean dish towel to keep warm.

Pop all the vegetables into the embers of the barbecue or hardwood fire. Turn occasionally and set aside when soft and slightly charred. The shallots, zucchini (courgette), and eggplant (aubergine) take the longest to cook—around 10–15 minutes.

To serve, slice the cooked vegetables, load into the flatbreads, and drizzle with the chermoula.

2

CAMPFIRES AND FIREPITS

Sitting around a campfire or firepit and chatting under the stars—is there anything more warming to the soul? Well, a few nice things to nibble on would help. If you have a fire going, then you may as well cook something on it. Campfire food should be simple and unfussy. You can cook most of the recipes in this chapter on a standard barbecue, too, but why not create a special repertoire for some quality time with family and friends around a fire?

Barbecue Campfire Beans

RECOMMENDED HEAT:
Medium-hot fire.

SERVES 6

1 red onion, diced

1 garlic clove, finely chopped

1 red bell (sweet) pepper, cored, deseeded, and diced

1 tbsp sunflower oil

2¼lb (1kg) smoked beef brisket (or pork) leftovers, cubed

14oz (400g) can pinto beans, drained

2 x 14oz (400g) can lima (butter) beans, drained

35oz (1kg) strained tomatoes (passata)

4 tbsp tomato ketchup

4 tbsp barbecue sauce

2 tbsp barbecue dry rub (just use your favorite)

1 tbsp American yellow mustard

3 tbsp cider vinegar

3 tbsp maple syrup

1 tbsp packed (soft) brown sugar

2 tsp hot sauce (such as Tabasco or similar)

Salt and freshly ground black pepper

To serve:

Crisp-skinned baked potatoes

If you're cooking lots of barbecue meats, you'll no doubt have leftovers at some point, so having a reliable barbecue beans recipe is a godsend. You can mix this up to suit your needs and riff off the basic recipe as you please. These campfire beans are a family favorite for using up leftover beef short ribs, pulled pork, and pork belly, or in this case, smoked beef brisket. Cooked in a Dutch oven or lidded flameproof dish over a firepit, you can leave this recipe ticking over for hours.

Soften the onion, garlic, and bell (sweet) pepper in the oil in the cooking bowl over the medium-hot fire for 10 minutes.

Add the cubed brisket or pork, and cook for a further 10 minutes.

Add the remainder of the ingredients, season to taste, and stir. Let cook for at least a couple of hours, preferably 4, with the lid on. Stir occasionally and top up with water or beer if the mixture gets too dry. Once cooked, the meat should be falling apart and tender, and the sauce nice and thick.

Enjoy your campfire beans on top of baked potatoes, or in a million other ways—the choice is yours.

Chimichurri Bread

RECOMMENDED HEAT:
Hot grill over a fire or a
wood-fired oven or smoker.

SERVES 2

Good-quality bread slices (at
least 4, more if you are hungry)

Softened butter (optional)

For the chimichurri:

Handful of fresh flat-leaf parsley

Handful of cilantro (fresh
coriander)

6 garlic cloves

1 small shallot, chopped

4–5 tbsp red wine vinegar

3 tbsp cold water

1 tsp coarse sea salt

1 tsp dried oregano

1 tsp red pepper (dried chili)
flakes

This has quickly become a family favorite and is often chosen over regular garlic bread—it's certainly great loaded up with grilled steaks. You have two ways of approaching this: simply brush some chimichurri on nice bread and then grill, as I have here, or stir the chimichurri into softened butter, spread on good bread, and cook in a wood-fired oven. If I'm grilling on a regular barbecue, I just brush on the chimichurri, but if I am cooking in a wood-fired oven, or in a smoker, then I mix the chimichurri with butter. The reason for this is that the extra fat from the butter would cause the coals to flare up and burn the bread on a barbecue.

Make up a batch of chimichurri by blitzing all the ingredients in a food processor or using a hand blender until you have a coarse paste.

Lavishly brush the slices of bread with the chimichurri, then place on the hot grill for a couple of minutes and toast on both sides.

If you are using a wood-fired oven or smoker, and mixing the chimichurri with butter, stir 1 teaspoon of chimichurri through 1 tablespoon of softened butter. Spread the butter over the slices of bread and cook in the oven or smoker until the bread is toasted and the chimichurri butter has melted.

Firepit Lamb Chops

RECOMMENDED HEAT:
Embers of a silver-birch fire
(ensuring the fire has been
going for a minimum of 2 hours
to build up a thick and even bed
of embers).

SERVES 1

2 lamb chops

Salt and freshly ground black
   pepper

For the herb baste:

2 sprigs each of fresh rosemary
   and thyme

Handful of fresh flat-leaf parsley

1 garlic clove

Juice of 1 lemon

1 tbsp coarse sea salt

¼ cup (60ml) extra-virgin
   olive oil

1 canned anchovy fillet (optional)

Cooking simple food over the embers of a wood fire in a firepit is a skill that should be learnt by any aspiring outdoor cook. Getting the heat to the right level is where the mastery of fire control comes into its own. Achieving the right type of heat is key—you need a good solid bed of embers to work with once the flames have died down, but before the coals have lost their edge. You want to sear and crisp up the fat on the meat without cremating it. For the herb baste used for these lamb chops, I included a single anchovy fillet. This is optional, but does make the baste taste better.

To make the herb baste, blitz all the ingredients together in a food processor or using a hand blender until you have a coarse paste.

Season the chops to taste and grill over the embers of the silver-birch fire, searing each side for a few minutes until caramelized. As you turn the chops, brush the hot surface with the herby baste.

Check the chops are cooked through to an internal temperature of 140°F (60°C)—you want them to be slightly pink and juicy.

Remove the chops from the grill and let rest with a little more baste brushed over before serving.

Smoked Leg of Lamb

RECOMMENDED HEAT:
Tripod over a fire bowl (in this case, a Kadai fire bowl), using a chain and hook to hang the leg of lamb over a gently smoldering, silver-birch fire. This method of cooking gives you a nice gentle to moderate heat and a wisp of smoke.

SERVES 6

Leg of lamb
For the salmuera:
2 cups (500ml) warm water
Sprig of fresh rosemary (optional)
Black peppercorns (optional)
1 garlic clove (optional)
Salt

I'm always very careful when I smoke lamb. A beautiful leg of salt marsh lamb, for example, only needs a delicate lick of gentle smoke and nothing more intense. My mate Olly brought this leg of lamb round for us to have a play with. I'd wanted to cook in this way for a while, and we had a great day cooking the lamb. We had planned a relaxing afternoon of cooking and enjoying some quality red wine, so wanted a nice easy cook—and firepit cooking is one of the most relaxed. The lamb is seasoned as it cooks with salmuera, which is a salt-water brine.

To make the salmuera, stir salt into the warm water in a pitcher (jug) until it reaches saturation point (the salt will stop dissolving). If you wish, add a sprig of rosemary, a few black peppercorns, and garlic for an extra hit of flavor. Let the salmuera cool and then funnel into a small plastic drinks bottle with a sports cap. You can then flick the salmuera over the meat while it cooks, to produce a lovely salty crust.

Hang the leg of lamb over the fire and start seasoning with the salmuera as it cooks.

Cook the lamb to an internal temperature of 140°F (60°C). This should take about 4–6 hours (to be honest, we lost track of time as the wine flowed). The cooking time will be influenced by the size of the leg, the fire temperature, and the air temperature, as well as any wind present. This is not precise barbecuing—this is using your senses and a good digital probe thermometer.

The smoke and salmuera form a lovely, slightly smoky crust on the outside of the lamb and the meat will be lovely, pink, and juicy inside—a real treat. Carve off some nice, thick, juicy slices and enjoy.

Campfire Chocolate Rolls

RECOMMENDED HEAT:
Moderate embers of a campfire or
barbecue at 350°F (180°C).

SERVES 4

4 soft cottage bread rolls
(or brioche rolls)

4 heaping tbsp chocolate
hazelnut spread

My kids go crazy for this recipe, and it's as simple as you can get. My wife and I like to make sure we get one as well. A cottage bread roll—a traditional style of roll that originated in England—makes the ideal container for the oozing melted chocolate: the little top knot pulls off easily, then you can scoop out the bread, fill with chocolate hazelnut spread, and pop the top back on. This can be achieved with other bread rolls by cutting into the top, but is less elegant.

A campfire or barbecue that has died down to embers is an ideal opportunity to make these rolls— you don't want flames, just a gentle heat to warm the rolls through.

Remove the top knot from the cottage rolls, or cut a hole in the top of the brioche rolls.

Use a teaspoon to hollow out a well inside each roll. Fill the well in each roll with a heaping tablespoon of chocolate hazelnut spread and pop the lids back.

Wrap each roll in a double layer of foil and place in the warm embers of the campfire or barbecue for around 10–15 minutes. Make sure the embers are not too hot, or the rolls will burn. You want the rolls to crisp up a little bit and the chocolate spread to be melted and runny.

To serve, unwrap the rolls and enjoy getting as messy as you like.

Pancakes with Maple Butter

RECOMMENDED HEAT:
Level bed of moderately hot embers of a campfire or barbecue at 350°F (180°C).

SERVES 4

For the pancake batter:
1¾ cups (200g) self-rising (raising) flour
1 US large (UK medium) egg
1½ cups (350ml) whole milk
1 tsp baking powder
2 tbsp plain (natural) yogurt
Pinch of fine sea salt
For the maple butter:
4 tbsp maple syrup (cold from the refrigerator)
4 tbsp (2oz/50g) unsalted butter, softened and almost melted, plus extra for frying

This recipe is a firm family favourite—my kids go wild for pancakes and maple syrup, especially when these are cooked outdoors on a campfire. I like to take things a bit further, though, and they love the theater of melting maple butter with a lump of charcoal over the top of a stack of fluffy pancakes. The charcoal caramelizes the maple syrup and melts the butter, so it drips down over the pancakes—heaven.

To make the maple butter, whisk the cold maple syrup into the butter in a bowl—the syrup will start to firm up the butter.

Cover the bowl of syrupy butter with plastic wrap (clingfilm), or form into a sausage shape and seal with plastic wrap. Pop in the refrigerator for a few hours to chill and firm up.

Meanwhile, make the pancake batter by whisking all the ingredients together in a pitcher (jug), and let rest for 30 minutes. You can get the campfire or barbecue ready at this stage.

Use a cast-iron skillet or pan, as the cast iron evens out the heat and makes for great pancakes. Melt a teaspoon of butter in the skillet or pan over the embers.

Use a ladle to pour a small amount of batter—to make a 4-inch (10cm) pancake— into the skillet or pan. Flip the pancake over when bubbles appear in the middle (this should only take a few minutes). The pancake should be nice and brown. Cook on the other side for a similar length of time. Remove to a plate, then repeat using the remainder of the batter and build up a stack of pancakes.

Cut a generous slice of the maple butter and place on top of each stack. You can just leave this to melt from the heat of the pancakes, but it's more fun to use a lump of red-hot charcoal from the embers of the fire. Just be sure you've used a good wood, such as silver birch, if you do this. Quickly place the burning charcoal on top of the butter—you'll get some nice smoke and a lovely, toffee-caramel smell. Remove the charcoal once the butter has melted, and serve.

3

CAST-IRON COOKING

Cooking in a cast-iron skillet or pan is a wonderful way to cook. After a period of aging and cooking, cast iron develops the best non-stick surface and a character all of its own. You can get cast iron screaming hot, and it also holds the heat for a long time. It is a great way to make butter sauces and glazes, and is also ideal if you want a lovely sauce finish—all you need is a nicely seasoned cast-iron skillet or pan and some heat.

Cast-iron Woodstove Pizzas

RECOMMENDED HEAT:
Heat a woodstove until it is good and hot using a hardwood such as silver birch—ideally to a temperature of 480–570°F (250–300°C). Add a couple of fresh logs, too, for some good heat.

MAKES 4

For the pizza bases:

18oz (500g) 00 bread flour, plus extra for dusting

¼oz (7g) instant dry yeast

Scant 1½ cups (325ml) water, at room temperature

½oz (10g) fine sea salt

For the pizza tomato sauce:

8 tbsp strained tomatoes (passata)

2 tsp red pesto

For the topping:

Mozzarella cheese (use the firm type and not the squishy one in the bag), sliced

Other toppings of your choice, including vegetables, cooked meat, and salami (I went for my favorite nduja)

I'm lucky to have a wood-fired oven, which I think is the best way of cooking a pizza—it's certainly the most authentic. I realize that not everyone has a wood-fired oven, but people often have a wood-burning stove in their front room, which can be used as a wood-fired oven of sorts in which to cook some nice pizzas. When cooking pizza in a woodstove, the key is to get a relatively balanced heat, and using a cast-iron skillet or pan works well here. I've experimented and found that preheating the pan too much often burns the bottom of the pizza before the top has crisped up. So I just warm it slightly for a minute, before adding the pizza base.

To make the pizza dough for the bases, add the flour, yeast, and water to a large mixing bowl and stir until well combined. Knead the dough, either by hand or using a food mixer with a dough hook, until it is silky smooth—this will take about 10 minutes. Cover the bowl with plastic wrap (clingfilm) and let rise in a warm place for a couple of hours or until the dough has doubled in size.

Split the dough into 4 equal-sized balls (each weighing about 3½oz/100g). Place the balls on a floured surface, cover with a clean dish towel, and let rise again in a warm place for an hour.

To make the pizza tomato sauce, mix the strained tomatoes (passata) and pesto in a bowl, and set aside.

Pre-warm a large, cast-iron skillet or pan. Stretch out one of the dough balls to the size of the skillet or pan and place in the pre-warmed pan. Spread some tomato sauce thinly over the pizza and top with the mozzarella and your choice of other toppings.

Place the skillet or pan in the woodstove, with the fire to the side. After a few minutes, spin the pan around 180 degrees and cook for a further few minutes. You may need to adjust the timings according to the thickness of the skillet or pan and the heat of the fire. My pizza took about 6 minutes. Repeat for the remaining balls of dough.

Indoor Barbecue Steak

RECOMMENDED HEAT:
Set up the woodstove with
a nice bed of red-hot embers
from a hardwood fire, such as
silver birch or oak.

SERVES 2

2 ribeye steaks or other steaks of
   your choice, each about 1 inch
   (2.5cm) thick
2 garlic cloves, halved
Sprig each of fresh rosemary and
   thyme
Pat (knob) of unsalted butter
Coarse sea salt and coarse black
   pepper

When the weather turns cooler in late fall (autumn), most people pack their barbecue away for the winter and light up their woodstove indoors. They don't seem to realize that they have lit a secret weapon in which they can cook some wonderful food. In the past, many homes (and a few still today) saw a woodstove as a way to cook as well as a means of providing warmth. When we moved into our house in the country in mid-winter, a delay in getting our new cooker installed meant we had a couple of weeks of cooking on a large old woodstove. This was a revelation to me, and since then I have always regarded the woodstove as my indoor barbecue. There is something wonderful about being able to cook with wood and fire when it's howling a gale and lashing down with rain outside (not that this will often stop me, though).

I like to cook a couple of steaks for a cozy steak dinner indoors. You can use a cast-iron griddle pan, as I have here, or, if you're feeling brave, cook an indoor "dirty" steak by cooking in the embers of a woodstove. An advantage of cooking in a woodstove is that the smoke goes straight up the chimney and you're not left with a smoky living room. There are many other dishes you can cook in or on a woodstove, so hopefully this will get you thinking of the possibilities if you are fortunate enough to have an indoor barbecue in your living room.

Get a cast-iron griddle pan nice and hot in the woodstove, then pop on the steaks. After a few minutes, add the halved garlic cloves and the herbs.

Flip the steaks after 4 minutes, and season the hot side with a pinch of sea salt and black pepper.

Cook for a further 3–4 minutes until the steaks are how you like them. For guidance on the internal temperature for rare, medium rare, well done, and so on, see the *Internal Temperature Guide* on page 13. I cooked these ribeye steaks to an internal temperature of 127°F (53°C), which increased to 130°F (55°C) after resting—this gave me a nice medium rare. Add a pat (knob) of butter to sizzle away for the last minute.

Once cooked, remove the steaks from the woodstove and rest for a few minutes, pouring over any juices from the pan and seasoning to taste with more sea salt and black pepper.

Serve with a nice glass of red, knowing you've cooked a great live-fire steak in your living room.

Sauté Potatoes with Padrón Peppers and Chorizo

RECOMMENDED HEAT:
Red-hot grill.

SERVES 2

14oz (400g) potatoes (such as pink fir apple or anya), peeled
5½oz (150g) Padrón peppers
½ chorizo ring, cut into coins
1 tbsp extra-virgin olive oil
Coarse sea salt

There are some wonderful flavors reminiscent of Spain in this dish. I really enjoy Padrón peppers grilled and then drizzled with olive oil and sea salt. In this recipe, I wanted to bring these together with some pan-fried chorizo and sauté potatoes. There's something special about crisping chorizo in a cast-iron skillet, with the rich, russet-colored oil that's released as the chorizo warms up, soaking into the gently sautéeing potatoes—the textures of this simple dish work really nicely together.

Cook the potatoes in a pan of boiling water until soft (about 10–12 minutes), then drain and slice into thick rounds. This can be done either on the grill or in the kitchen, if that is easier.

Pop the peppers on the red-hot grill and cook until they start to char and blister—this should only take a minute or two.

Place the peppers in a cast-iron skillet or pan with the potatoes, chorizo, and olive oil, and return to the grill. Sauté over a high heat until the potatoes are just starting to crisp up.

Sprinkle the potatoes with sea salt and serve.

SAUTÉ POTATOES WITH PADRÓN PEPPERS AND CHORIZO

Skillet Meatballs with Tomato Sauce

RECOMMENDED HEAT:
Medium-hot grill, with a couple of chunks of cherry wood on the charcoal to create a nice smoke.

SERVES 4

4 tbsp barbecue dry rub (such as CountryWoodSmoke House Rub)

2¼lb (1kg) ground (minced) steak

For the tomato sauce:

2 cups (500ml) strained tomatoes (passata)

About ⅓ cup (125ml) barbecue sauce of your choice

3 tbsp barbecue dry rub

4 tsp Worcestershire sauce

Handful of grated Cheddar cheese

To serve:

Cooked white rice

Toasted garlic bread or Chimichurri Bread (see page 39)

Pickled sliced jalapeños

Small handful of chopped cilantro (fresh coriander)

I love grilling something and then popping it in a cast-iron skillet or pan with some sauce—you get the smoke and sear of the direct heat, and can then add flavors with your choice of sauce. Here, the combination of cherry-wood-smoked meatballs smothered with a tomato sauce and some cheese showcases this method at its best.

Firstly, make the meatball mix by kneading the dry rub into the ground (minced) steak until evenly combined. Shape the ground steak into golf-ball-sized meatballs, rolling the balls in the palms of your hands until they are nice and smooth.

Grill the meatballs on the medium-hot grill until nicely seared on the outside. You want a nice golden brown color, which should take 8–10 minutes.

Stir all the tomato sauce ingredients, except the cheese, together in a pitcher (jug).

Pop the meatballs in a cast-iron skillet or pan, pour over the tomato sauce, and sprinkle the Cheddar cheese over the top.

Cook over the charcoal with the lid on until the sauce bubbles, the cheese melts, and the meatballs reach an internal temperature of 165°F (74°C). This should take around 30 minutes.

Serve with some cooked white rice and nicely toasted garlic or Chimichurri Bread, adding a few pickled sliced jalapeños and a sprinkling of cilantro (fresh coriander) on top.

Pork with Lemon, Honey, and Thyme

RECOMMENDED HEAT:
Set up a barbecue with a level bed of medium-hot embers, or use a wood-fired oven heated to a temperature of 400°F (200°C).

SERVES 2

14–18oz (400–500g) pork tenderloin, cut into 1¼-inch (3cm) cubes

1 lemon, quartered

2 sprigs of fresh thyme

Pinch each of coarse sea salt and ground black pepper

2 tsp runny honey

The flavors in this dish are more than the sum of their parts when cooked in the searing heat of a cast-iron skillet or pan. The pork caramelizes in the heat and is glazed with lemon juice and sweet honey, while the thyme adds just the right amount of herby background to make the whole dish sing.

Put a cast-iron skillet or pan in the barbecue (either on the grill or on top of the embers) or wood-fired oven to warm up. Add the cubed pork, three of the lemon quarters, and the thyme. Season with the sea salt and black pepper, then sear the outside of the pork until it is nicely browned—this should take about 4–5 minutes.

Squeeze the fourth of the lemon quarters over the pork and drizzle with the honey.

Cook the pork for a few more minutes until the internal temperature reaches 145°F (63°C). This ensures the pork remains juicy and slightly pink, and does not dry out.

Cast-iron Peaches

RECOMMENDED HEAT:
Heat a wood-fired oven to a temperature of around 400°F (200°C)—you want a gentle flame to lick the tops of the peaches. Alternatively, set up a barbecue for moderate direct cooking with the lid on.

SERVES 2

2 perfectly ripe peaches, halved and pitted (stoned)

2 tsp turbinado (demerara) sugar

2 tbsp pumpkin seeds

Sprinkle of fresh thyme leaves

To serve:

Cream or ice cream

Stone fruits, such as peaches, are a great way to end a meal of rich barbecue food—they are light and zingy, and can refresh a jaded palate. They are wonderful grilled, but I love them cooked simply in a cast-iron pan in a wood-fired oven or woodstove, where you get a searing heat from above, which chars and caramelizes the tops, and heat from below that softens the juicy flesh. There's no need to be fancy here: as simple things go, these are sublime. The pumpkin seeds offer a nice element of toasty crunch. These peaches can also be cooked on a barbecue set up for moderate direct cooking—you just need to char and caramelize them on both sides.

Place the peach halves, cut-side facing up, in a cast-iron skillet or pan. Sprinkle the sugar evenly over the cut surface, then dust with the pumpkin seeds and thyme leaves.

Cook the peaches in the wood-fired oven, or on the barbecue with the lid on, for around 15–20 minutes, or until the peaches soften and the tops are charred and caramelized. If you're using a barbecue, place the peaches, cut-side facing down, on the grill to caramelize on that side first, then turn them over halfway through the cooking time to caramelize on the other side. Make sure the pumpkin seeds don't burn, but just toast off.

Serve warm with your choice of cream or ice cream.

4

GRILLING

Some foods need a direct heat treatment, but might be a little delicate or fatty for cooking directly on the coals. In general, the smaller and thinner the food, the hotter the coals need to be to stop the food drying out. You can grill small yakitori skewers over screaming-hot coals, or gently grill chunks of meat, turning occasionally on a parilla or Tuscan grill over gently smoldering embers. All you really need is some embers to cook on, something to contain them, and a grill grate. My preference is cast iron as it holds the heat better—ideally, the closer to the coals, the better. If the food sticks to the grates, leave it a while longer and it will start to release itself as the seared crust develops.

Grilled Chicken Thighs with Pickled White Barbecue Sauce

RECOMMENDED HEAT:
Set up a barbecue for
medium-hot (320–350°F/
160–180°C), direct grilling,
with a chunk of hickory or cherry
wood to smoke.

SERVES 1

2 boneless chicken thighs,
  skin-on

2 tsp barbecue dry rub
  (such as CountryWoodSmoke
  House Rub)

*For the pickled white barbecue
sauce:*

6 tbsp good-quality mayonnaise

2 tbsp cider vinegar

3 pickled gherkins, finely diced

1 tbsp pickle juice (from the jar
  of pickled gherkins)

1 tbsp American yellow mustard

1 tsp white sugar

1 garlic clove, mashed to a pulp

1 tsp creamed horseradish

2 tsp coarsely ground black
  pepper

Good pinch of sea salt

To serve:

Selection of pickles, such as
  sliced jalapeños and gherkins

I was set a bit of a challenge at a recent demo by a chef friend of mine, to come up with a new twist on the humble grilled chicken thighs that I often cook, and which are a real family favorite. So this was the outcome. Alabama white sauce is relatively unknown here in the UK, which is a real shame, as it goes so well with poultry, such as chicken and turkey. I love it, but wanted to give it a little CountryWoodSmoke twist…

Make the sauce in advance by mixing all the ingredients together in a bowl.

Remove the bones from the chicken thighs, if necessary. Boneless chicken thighs are flatter and cook more evenly, while the skin also crisps up better.

Sprinkle the dry rub lightly and evenly over the thighs, on both the skin and meat side.

Cook the thighs, skin-side facing down, on the grill for around 10–15 minutes, to render the fat and crisp up the skin. Turn the thighs over and cook for a further 5 minutes, ensuring the internal temperature has reached 165°F (74°C).

Serve the chicken thighs with a drizzle of the barbecue sauce, and a few pickles on the side. (Cover any unused sauce and store in the refrigerator, it should keep for a week.)

GRILLED CHICKEN THIGHS WITH PICKLED WHITE BARBECUE SAUCE

Grilled Lamb Leg Steaks with Chamomile Salsa Verde

RECOMMENDED HEAT:
Red-hot grill using lump charcoal.

SERVES 2

2 lamb leg steaks

Sea salt and freshly cracked black pepper

For the chamomile salsa verde:

Large handful of chamomile fronds and flowers, plus extra to garnish (optional)

1 garlic clove

Scant ¼ cup (50ml) good-quality extra-virgin olive oil

Juice of ½ lemon

Good pinch of sea salt

To serve:

New potatoes

This recipe came about while I was cooking for a wonderful friend of mine, Jan, who runs Maddocks Farm, in Devon, England, and grows the most amazing edible flowers. The dish was for a special party and I cooked a whole lamb stuffed with herbs in a Cajun microwave. I had decided on a herby salsa verde to serve with the lamb. I was wandering around the herbs Jan grows and happened upon a large patch of chamomile—the grassy, herby taste of the fronds and flowers make a superbly fragrant salsa verde. You can serve the salsa verde with a whole lamb or, as I have here, a couple of lovely, juicy lamb leg steaks grilled over charcoal.

Make the salsa verde in advance by blitzing up all the ingredients in a food processor or using a hand blender until you have a coarse paste. Set aside.

Season the lamb leg steaks with a pinch of sea salt and grill for approximately 4 minutes on each side, ensuring the meat reaches an internal temperature 140°F (60°C) for medium and is still blushing pink. If you prefer your lamb more rare or well done, see the *Internal Temperature Guide* on page 13).

Remove the lamb steaks from the barbecue and let rest for a couple of minutes. Sprinkle with a pinch of black pepper just before serving.

To serve, drizzle with a little of the chamomile salsa verde and garnish with a few spare chamomile fronds and flowers (optional). We enjoyed ours with some home-grown new potatoes.

GRILLED LAMB LEG STEAKS WITH CHAMOMILE SALSA VERDE

Grilled Eggplant Steaks with Miso and Honey Glaze

RECOMMENDED HEAT:
Red-hot grill using
lump charcoal.

SERVES 2

1 large eggplant
  (aubergine)
Sprinkle of red pepper
  (dried chili) flakes
  (optional)
Sea salt
*For the miso and honey
glaze:*
1 tsp miso paste (any color
  will work)
1 tsp runny honey
2 tsp mirin
1 tsp soy sauce
2 tsp toasted sesame oil
To serve:
Steamed jasmine rice

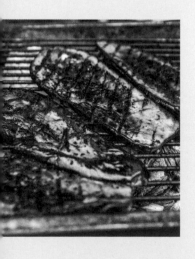

Bear with me all you meat-lovers... this is really good. I do love a nice steak but, as some of you know, I was a vegetarian for 14 years, and I clearly remember going to barbecues and getting palmed off with dry and lifeless veggie burgers and other vegetarian fare. Usually the most exciting thing would be some grilled vegetable kebabs. Well, I admit there's not very much on these pages for vegetarians, so I thought I'd include this wonderful recipe to balance things out. Eggplants (aubergines) are wonderful chargrilled over charcoal; they are sponges for flavor and work so well when grilled. I opted for a Japanese-inspired Miso and Honey Glaze on these eggplant steaks.

Eggplant, known as aubergine in the UK, is a great blank canvas for flavor, but needs a little preparation. Slice the eggplant lengthwise into steaks, ¾ inch (2cm) thick. Sprinkle both sides with a little sea salt and let sit on a plate for an hour. Removing the slightly bitter juices in this way gives you a great-tasting eggplant.

Wipe any excess salt or moisture from the eggplant steaks, and score very slightly with a sharp knife in a crisscross pattern across both sides.

Mix all the ingredients for the glaze together in a bowl until fully combined.

Brush the glaze generously over both sides of each eggplant steak, leaving a little of the glaze left to brush on at the end.

Cook on the red-hot grill for a few minutes on each side—you're looking for the eggplant to soften a little without becoming mushy and the surface to caramelize nicely without burning.

Once softened and nicely charred, brush the steaks with the remaining glaze. I also like to sprinkle mine with some red pepper (dried chili) flakes.

Serve on a bed of steamed jasmine rice. Certainly a step up from cardboard veggie burgers.

Grilled Garlic Scapes

RECOMMENDED HEAT:
Red-hot grill using lump charcoal.
I used a Japanese-style hibachi
grill with oak lump charcoal.

SERVES 1

Handful of garlic scapes

Drizzle of sesame oil

Sprinkling of togarashi pepper
spice

To serve:

1 red or orange bell (sweet)
pepper, halved, cored,
and deseeded

Steamed jasmine rice

Garlic scapes (the young flowerheads of garlic) can be abundant during late spring and early summer, when the soil begins to warm up and the garlic tries to flower. If you leave the plants to flower, they take energy from the bulb, so the scapes are removed before the plant flowers. Scapes are wonderful grilled over a charcoal grill. They are like a kind of garlicy asparagus and one of my favorite things to eat. I just wish I could get more of them.

Drizzle the scapes with sesame oil and sprinkle with a little togarashi pepper spice.

Cook the scapes on the red-hot grill—you'll find that they pop and crackle. Cook the scapes until they develop a lovely char.

Grill the bell (sweet) pepper until it softens and chars slightly.

Serve the grilled scapes with the grilled pepper and steamed jasmine rice for a healthy but delicious meal.

Grilled Red Mullet
with Pea Shoot Cream

RECOMMENDED HEAT:
Red-hot grill using lump charcoal.

SERVES 1

Olive oil, for brushing

2–3 small red mullet

Coarse sea salt and freshly ground black pepper

For the pea shoot cream:

2 tbsp crème fraîche

2 small handfuls of pea shoots

Squeeze of fresh lemon

To serve:

2 slices of good-quality bread (such as rye sourdough)

2 handfuls of pea shoots

Couple of slices of fresh lemon

When I visited my local fishmonger in Devon to pick up the ingredients for a grilled fish dish I had a totally different recipe in my mind, involving mackerel and fennel. But I spotted these beautiful red mullet and the price was too hard to resist. Hopefully, you won't mind missing out on the mackerel recipe. If you haven't tried red mullet, then you really should—it is one of my favorite fish to cook on the grill, having a wonderful, subtle, shellfish-like flavor when super-fresh, plus the skin crisps up to make one of the nicest things I've eaten. These mullet were lovely, small, and plump, around the same size as sardines, but coral-pink in color. While shopping, I also noticed some fresh pea shoots, and so knocked together a creamy, pea-flavored sauce to drizzle over the top. This worked a treat, as the sauce was delicate and didn't overpower the subtle and amazing flavor of the red mullet.

Make the cream sauce in advance by blitzing the crème fraîche, pea shoots, and squeeze of lemon in a food processor or using a hand blender. Taste and check the sauce has a subtle taste of pea and lemon. If not, add some more pea shoots and lemon juice, until you are happy with the flavor.

Brush the grates of the grill and the skin of each mullet with a little olive oil, and season to taste with sea salt and black pepper. Cook for a few minutes on each side, ensuring the mullet reach an internal temperature of 145°F (63°C) and that the skin is nice and crisp.

Pop the slices of bread on the grill to toast slightly.

To serve, place the pea shoots and red mullet on top of the toasted bread and drizzle over the pea shoot cream. Garnish with the lemon slices.

RECOMMENDED HEAT:
Set up a barbecue for moderate (285–320°F/140–160°C), direct grilling using lump charcoal. Adding a chunk of fruitwood, such as apple or cherry, to the coals will give the halloumi a lovely, gentle, smoky flavor.

SERVES 2

8oz (225g) block of halloumi

1 tbsp olive oil

For the chermoula:

1 red chili pepper

2 large garlic cloves

Handful of cilantro (fresh coriander)

6 tbsp extra-virgin olive oil

2 tbsp white wine vinegar

Juice of 1 lemon

2 tsp paprika

2 tsp ground cumin

Pinch of sea salt

For the rosemary flatbreads:

1 cup (125g) all-purpose (plain) flour, plus extra for dusting

5 tbsp (75ml) warm water

½ tbsp olive oil

½ tsp fine sea salt

Sprig of fresh rosemary, leaves removed and finely chopped

To serve:

Handful of cilantro (fresh coriander)

Handful of fresh flat-leaf parsley

Grilled Halloumi in Rosemary Flatbreads

There's something a bit special about the way halloumi grills over hot coals: the surface browns and crisps, intensifying the lovely saltiness of the cheese, while the inside puffs up and loses its squeakiness. It's honestly one of my favorite grilled foods. Halloumi takes on smoke well, too, so you can grill and smoke to get the best out of it. Serve with crisp rosemary flatbreads and fragrant chermoula drizzled over the top, and you have a real winner.

Prepare the chermoula in advance by blitzing all the ingredients in a food processor or using a hand blender until you have a loose paste. Add more olive oil, if required.

To prepare the flatbreads, mix all the ingredients together in a bowl, either by hand or using a food mixer with a dough hook, until you have a smooth dough. Knead the dough for 8–10 minutes. Pop the dough in the bowl, cover with plastic wrap (clingfilm), and let rest for 20–30 minutes at room temperature.

Split the dough into four equal pieces. Dust your work surface with a little flour. Roll the flatbreads into rough rounds using a rolling pin.

Bake the flatbreads on the hot grill or hot coals of the barbecue for a few minutes on each side, or until just charred and crisped up in places. Set aside and wrap in a clean dish towel to keep warm.

Cut the halloumi block in half horizontally, so you have two large, flat squares—this maximizes the surface area and ensures the halloumi cooks through and is less "squeaky." Brush on both sides with the olive oil and place on the grill.

Cook the slices of halloumi for around 5–6 minutes on each side. You want the halloumi to start to char a little and turn a lovely golden brown. It will also start to puff up a little once any water cooks off. Make sure the halloumi is cooked nicely on both sides.

Serve the halloumi in slices on the flatbreads, with a little cilantro (fresh coriander) and flat-leaf parsley, then drizzle generously with the chermoula.

+

GRILL TIPS

You could try substituting the chermoula for some chimichurri (see page 39) or my Dirty baste (see page 22) for an equally wonderful taste.

Pulled Fennel and Halloumi Burger

RECOMMENDED HEAT:
Set up a barbecue for low-moderate (250–300°F/120–150°C), direct grilling. You'll need a lump of pear wood for the smoked halloumi. You can also use a smoker with a lid for the pear-smoked halloumi.

SERVES 2

1 fennel bulb, sliced lengthwise to keep the root intact

1 tbsp (15g) butter

8oz (225g) block of halloumi

To serve:

2 good-quality wholegrain bread rolls

2 tsp chili jam

Chili sauce, such as Sriracha (optional)

I'll hold my hand up—I have neglected vegetarian barbecue food. I do love vegetarian food, but don't think it should be classed as something different or limited to store-bought veggie burgers and sausages on the barbecue. I had been looking for a vegetarian alternative to the ubiquitous pulled pork that was not only acceptable, but really rather fabulous, and I think this pulled fennel is it. When slow-roasted over charcoal and basted with melted butter, sliced fennel becomes sweet and juicy, with a lovely charred flavor. The flavors in this burger work so well: the sweet, smoky, slightly aniseed-y fennel; the salty, crisp, and soft halloumi; and the sweet heat hit from the chili jam. This might be the best vegetarian burger ever—and I'm sure will be enjoyed by the most committed of carnivores.

Pop a lump of pear wood on low-moderate barbecue coals, or in a smoker with a lid, to start smoking. Hot-smoke (see Techniques, page 11) the halloumi for around 40 minutes.

Meanwhile slowly char the slices of fennel bulb on a low-moderate grill for 20–30 minutes until sticky and sweet. Baste the fennel with the butter every now and then. The bulb should fall apart into lovely strands.

Slice the pear-smoked halloumi lengthwise down the long edge and pop on the grill next to the fennel until crisp on the outside and soft inside. When cooked well in this way, halloumi loses its squeaky texture and yet stays nice and firm on the grill.

To assemble the burgers, divide the buns between two plates. Add a tablespoon of chili jam to the bottom half of each bun, spreading to the edges with the back of a spoon. Follow with half of the fennel, one piece of hallomi, an extra squirt of chili sauce (if you like it hot), and the other half of the bun. Serve immediately and enjoy.

Charred Chicory with Honey, Chili, and Blue Cheese

RECOMMENDED HEAT:
As you are cooking over direct heat on a red-hot grill, set the grate 1–2 inch (2.5–5cm) above the coals.

SERVES 1

1–2 chicory heads

Drizzle of olive oil

2 tbsp crumbled blue cheese (such as dolcelatte or Cornish blue)

1 tsp runny honey

Pinch of red pepper (dried chili) flakes

Chicory (also known as endive) is a wonderful vegetable; it is crisp and refreshing, with a slightly bitter edge. It grills well over a high heat, charring a little and gaining a slightly sweet depth of flavor, while still retaining crispness. Grilled chicory can be eaten in many ways, perhaps served with a nice creamy sauce or dressed with olive oil and balsamic vinegar. Or accompanied, as here, with a few complementary ingredients, including blue cheese for a bit of funky creaminess—dolcelatte is a good option, but I went for some Cornish blue. The honey adds just the right sweetness, while the red pepper (dried chili) flakes give a little kick for extra interest.

Cut the chicory into quarters lengthwise, keeping the root intact to hold the leaves together.

Drizzle a little olive oil over the chicory leaves, and rub in. Grill the chicory over the hot coals until slightly charred on all sides, turning as required.

Place the chicory in a serving dish. Crumble over the blue cheese, drizzle with the runny honey, and sprinkle over the red pepper (dried chili) flakes.

Enjoy the charred chicory alone, or as a great side dish with pork (and many other dishes).

5

ROTISSERIE AND SKEWERS

To everything: turn, turn, turn... turning pieces of meat in front of or over a fire has a great history—large spits with chunks of roasting meat are a part of the British heritage of cooking, larding and basting, and building up levels of flavor. This method of cooking can keep food moister and create a lovely even crust. You can buy beautiful, antique clockwork rotisserie, or use a modern battery-powered affair. I have cooked everything from chickens up to whole pigs on rotating spits. There are plenty of designs available, depending on how heavy your food is. For little skewers, you can get amazing, auto-rotating, Greek skewer grills, or you can simply turn the skewers yourself.

Bay-skewered Lamb

RECOMMENDED HEAT:
Medium-hot embers.

SERVES 2

2 lamb neck fillets
2 tbsp ras el hanout seasoning

I love lamb that is simply flavored, skewered, and then cooked over hot embers. If you get the heat right, you can give the lamb a lovely char while keeping the meat juicy and slightly pink. You could, of course, go for metal or wooden skewers, but I had a bay tree that needed a little pruning and so I used stalks from that. Woody rosemary stalks also work well, as do the young shoots of fruit trees such as apple or pear. As the skewer warms up and chars a little, this adds a wonderfully fragrant flavor to the meat.

Whittle the ends of the woody shoots to a point so that you can push them through the meat—the points need to be relatively sharp. Trim off any leaves or twigs.

Cut the neck fillets into ¾–1¼-inch (2–3cm) cubes, then push the cubes onto the skewers and dust with the ras el hanout seasoning.

Grill the skewered lamb over the medium-hot embers until the outside is charred and the meat has an internal temperature of 150°F (65°C). Serve and enjoy.

Lamb and Shallot Skewers

RECOMMENDED HEAT:
Set up a grill using red-hot lump charcoal for moderate to high direct cooking.

SERVES 4

1lb 10oz (750g) lamb neck fillet, cut into 1¼-inch (3cm) cubes

6–8 shallots, halved

For the shawarma spice mix:

1 tbsp ground coriander

1 tsp dried oregano

1 tsp ground allspice

1 tsp ground cinnamon

1 tsp ground cumin

1 tsp garlic powder

½ tsp ground ginger

½ tsp ground turmeric

½ tsp freshly ground black pepper

½ tsp chili powder (optional, if you like it hot)

1 tsp salt

To serve:

Flatbreads, salad, plain (natural) yogurt, tahini, and Sriracha chili sauce (optional), or cooked rice or couscous

A good lamb skewer cooked over coals until the fat crisps up is pretty special. Lamb fat crisps up and takes on every subtle nuance of smoke and dry rub. Here, I use a wonderfully fragrant blend of Middle Eastern spices, a kind of shawarma spice mix. This works really nicely with the grilled lamb, while the charred shallots add a sweet caramelized flavor to the mix.

Alternately push cubes of lamb and shallots on metal skewers—¼-inch (5mm) wide skewers are ideal.

Mix all the ingredients for the shawarma spice mix in a bowl, then sprinkle it over the skewers.

Start searing the skewers over direct heat on the grill, turning occasionally so the food doesn't burn—a little char is fine, though. Each skewer should take 8–10 minutes to cook, and the lamb should hit an internal temperature of 140°F (60°C) and remain slightly pink.

Enjoy the lamb skewers with some nice flatbreads, salad, yogurt, and tahini. A spicy sauce, such as Sriracha chili sauce, also works well. Alternatively, serve as part of a main meal with cooked rice or couscous.

Rotisserie Tandoori Chicken

RECOMMENDED HEAT:
Medium-hot rotisserie grill
at around 320°F (160°C).

SERVES 4

1 large whole chicken

Coarse sea salt

For the marinade:

8 tbsp plain (natural) yogurt

2 tsp beetroot powder

2 tsp tandoor spice mix

2 tsp garam masala

Good pinch of coarse sea salt

Juice of 1 lime

To serve:

Cooked basmati rice

Selection of Indian condiments
(such as mango chutney, chili
sauce, and lime pickle)

When a chicken starts spinning, a special magic appears to take place. The meat cooks through evenly, gets crispy skin, and stays super-moist. A centrifugal force seems to keep the juices from escaping. A simple rotisserie chicken hot off the grill is indeed something special, but here I've gone for a fragrant yogurt marinade in order to approximate the effect of a true tandoor oven.

Make the marinade by mixing together the yogurt, beetroot powder, tandoor spice mix, garam masala, sea salt, and lime juice.

Slash into the thighs of the chicken with a sharp knife. Coat the whole bird with the marinade, popping a couple of tablespoons inside the cavity as well. Cover with plastic wrap (clingfilm) and put in the refrigerator for at least a few hours, or preferably overnight.

Remove the chicken from the refrigerator and sprinkle over a couple of good pinches of sea salt.

Secure the chicken to the rotisserie and cook until the skin starts to become crispy and charred on the edges. You are looking at just over an hour for a medium chicken, but make sure the internal temperature of the thickest part of the thigh reaches 165°F (74°C).

Remove the chicken from the rotisserie and let rest under foil for around 15–20 minutes. You can either leave the chicken on the rotisserie while it's resting, or remove it.

While the chicken is resting, prepare some sides. I usually go for basmati rice and a selection of Indian condiments, such as mango chutney, chili sauce, and lime pickle.

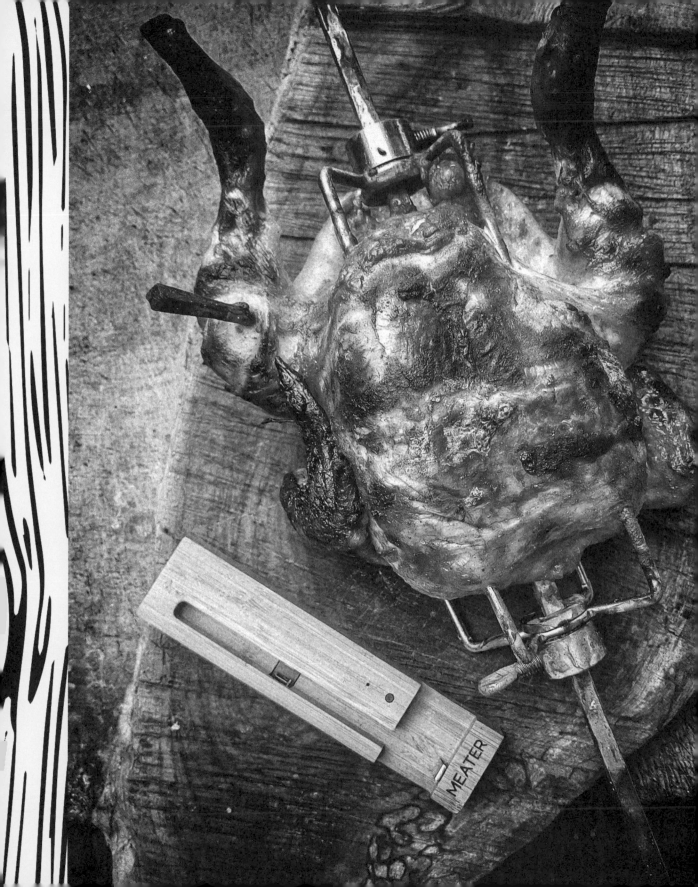

Glazed Chicken, Bacon, and Avocado Skewers

RECOMMENDED HEAT:
Set up a grill with red-hot lump charcoal for direct cooking.

SERVES 2

10 slices streaky bacon

1 large ripe (but not overly ripe) avocado, cut into roughly 1¼-inch (3cm) pieces

2 skinless chicken breasts, cut into 1¼-inch (3cm) cubes

Sea salt and freshly ground black pepper

For the glaze:

2 tbsp runny honey

2 tsp Sriracha chili sauce

To serve:

Warm wraps or submarine rolls

Extra Sriracha chili sauce

Many people are surprised that you can grill avocadoes, but it definitely works well—the edges char up and the flesh takes on a good flavor from any charcoal smoke. Wrap the chunks of avocado in crispy bacon, and you're onto a winner. You can glaze with whatever works for you, but this honey and Sriracha chili sauce glaze is a treat.

Mix together the honey and chili sauce for the glaze, then set aside.

Cut the slices of bacon in half and wrap around the avocado pieces.

Get your skewers, ideally metal skewers that are ¼ inch (5mm) in diameter, and alternately thread the cubes of chicken and bacon-wrapped avocado pieces onto the skewers. Season lightly—a pinch of sea salt and black pepper on each skewer should suffice.

Grill the skewers on the red-hot grill, turning as necessary. Ensure the chicken reaches an internal temperature of 165°F (74°C)— it should take 8–10 minutes to cook and be slightly crispy on the edges.

Brush the skewers evenly with the glaze, before grilling for the last couple of minutes.

Serve the skewers in warm wraps or submarine rolls with some extra Sriracha chili sauce.

Japanese Barbecue
Beef Skewers

RECOMMENDED HEAT:
Get the grill as hot as you can,
ideally using one with cast-iron
grill bars. Oil the grates with
a little rapeseed oil so the food
doesn't stick—to do this, I use
a folded piece of paper towel
soaked with a little oil and held
with barbecue tongs.

SERVES 2

18oz (500g) dry-aged fillet steak

4 large flat-cap mushrooms,
    washed and stems removed

6 tbsp hibachi grilling sauce or
    teriyaki sauce

To serve:

Steamed rice

Cooking over charcoal is popular the world over; so many cultures love the taste and smokiness of cooking food, however briefly, on the dry searing heat of charcoal. In Japan, hibachi are little ceramic pots that contain charcoal to cook on, and the Japanese barbecue style of cooking small skewers such as yakitori (bite-size meat or fish) is a great one. Hibachi grills are what we in the West understand by the term hibachi: little heavy iron grills that can reach a super-hot temperature. Perfect for cooking fillet-steak skewers. The quality of the beef here is critical, so go and talk to your friendly butcher. I went for a beautiful, dry-aged Aberdeen Angus chateaubriand.

This is simplicity itself to put together. Cut the steak and mushrooms into 1-inch (2.5cm) thick slices. Push the meat and mushrooms onto metal or wooden skewers and brush on the hibachi or teriyaki sauce. I like to use double-pronged or flat skewers to stop the food from rolling around.

Cook the skewers on the hot grill for 2–3 minutes on one side. The sugars in the sauce will caramelize and add to the rich umami flavor. Turn the skewers and cook for a further 2–3 minutes on the other side—the meat needs to be rare.

Serve with a bowl of steamed rice. ·

Nduja-stuffed Porchetta

RECOMMENDED HEAT:
Medium-hot rotisserie grill at
around 400°F (200°C).

FEEDS A CROWD

4½lb (2kg) pork belly,
  skin-on and boneless
7oz (200g) nduja
Few good pinches of coarse
  sea salt

Porchettas are a wonderful thing, and to my mind are best cooked on a rotisserie—in fact, I think they are probably one of the best things you can cook on a rotisserie. The magic of using a rotisserie is that the skin is alternately exposed to a hot side and a cooler side, which crisps up the skin and produces heavenly crackling. Porchettas are often stuffed with herbs, garlic, and lemon. I stuffed mine with some of my mate Mark's amazing nduja from the Duchy Charcuterie in Cornwall, England. If you haven't heard of nduja, it's a spicy, fatty spreadable salami from Calabria, in Italy. When heated, nduja adds a rich, spicy fat to anything it touches; it's perfect for a porchetta stuffing. I went for a pork belly for this porchetta, which is very rich.

Leave the pork belly overnight in the refrigerator with the skin exposed to dehydrate—this will help the crackling form.

Remove the pork belly from the refrigerator and spread the inside with the nduja. Roll up the porchetta, removing the excess skin (you don't want skin on the inside of the porchetta, or it won't crisp up).

Tie the porchetta with butcher's slip knots using heavy butcher's twine to keep it secure—you should now have a nice, barrel-shaped porchetta. (Look on YouTube to see how to tie a butcher's slip knot.)

Score the skin of the pork with a sharp knife in between the pieces of tied string and rub liberally with coarse sea salt, working this into the scores on the skin.

Slide the porchetta onto the rotisserie, using the prongs to secure it in place. Cook the porchetta on the rotisserie for a couple of hours. The skin should form nice crackling. The internal temperature should reach at least 185°F (85°C) and a skewer should go into the meat like butter.

Remove the porchetta from the spit, and let rest for 15–20 minutes.

Cut the porchetta into thick slices and serve with the crackling.

Rotisserie Beef Topside with Creamy Horseradish

RECOMMENDED HEAT:
Hot rotisserie grill at around 350–400°F (180–200°C) with the charcoal banked up to one side and, ideally, not directly below the beef (otherwise the dripping fat will flare up). Sprinkle a handful of oak chips over the coals or add a single chunk of oak to smoke.

SERVES 4–5

3lb 5oz (1.5kg) rolled beef topside

Plenty of coarse sea salt and freshly cracked black pepper

For the creamy horseradish:

4 tbsp crème fraîche

4 tsp creamed horseradish (or, ideally, freshly grated horseradish)

To serve:

Good-quality bread, thickly sliced

Arugula (rocket) or watercress

A solid beef sandwich is an important dish to have in your barbecue armory. All you need is some really good bread, good beef, and some hot horseradish to go alongside. When teaching my barbecue basics class, this is one of the things I like to demonstrate—a lovely barbecued topside of beef, with a hint of smoke and lots of sea salt and cracked black pepper. Best served rare and cut into thin slivers.

Season the beef generously with sea salt and black pepper—be more liberal with the seasoning than feels right. Secure the beef on the rotisserie.

Set the rotisserie going and cook the beef for around 40 minutes–1 hour, checking the internal temperature reaches 125°F (52°C). By the time the beef has rested, the temperature will have increased to 130°F (55°C) and the meat will be a nice medium rare. It's best not to cook topside of beef past medium, otherwise it will be tough and dry.

Remove the beef from the barbecue and let rest until the internal temperature reaches 130°F (55°C)—this will take about 20–30 minutes. You can either leave the beef on the rotisserie while it's resting, or remove it.

While the beef is resting, mix the crème fraîche with the horseradish in a bowl and set aside.

To serve, carve the beef and place on thick slices of bread with a handful of arugula (rocket) and some creamy horseradish.

Barbecue Goat Picanha with Chimichurri Rojo

RECOMMENDED HEAT:
Set up a grill using hot lump charcoal with a gap in the middle—that is, with coals on either side so there will be none directly under the meat. This stops the fat flaring up as it starts to crisp; otherwise you will have a raging inferno on your hands.

SERVES 4–6

4½lb (2kg) goat rump (picanha)

Coarse sea salt

For the chimichurri rojo:

2 garlic cloves

½ red onion

Handful each of fresh flat-leaf parsley and oregano

About ½ cup (125ml) olive oil

1 tbsp tomato paste (purée)

Splash of red wine vinegar

Good pinch of coarse sea salt

Pinch of smoked paprika

4–6 red bell (sweet) peppers, cored, deseeded, and quartered

To serve:

Green salad

I had a lovely piece of billy meat from friends who raise ex-dairy goats for meat in Devon where I live. I had previously cooked a delicious rack of their goat meat and wanted to do something with a lovely slab of their goat rump using a bit more direct heat. Picanha is a rump cut of beef, sometimes called sirloin cap or rump cap, which has a ridge of creamy fat on the upper side. I decided to cook the goat rump in a similar way to how fat-capped picanha is often cooked in Brazil: with the cap of fat exposed, so that I could crisp it up. Cabrito (roasted "kid" goat) is also very popular in Brazil. So, although this recipe uses a slab of goat rump, it is cooked in the same way as picanha with the slab of fat on top. The chimichurri rojo is a red version of green chimichurri (see page 39).

Make the chimichurri rojo by blitzing all the ingredients in a food processor or using a hand blender until you have a smooth-ish paste. Loosen the paste with a little more olive oil if you wish.

Cut the rump into thick slices and bend these round onto two thick metal skewers to hold the meat in place (see photo). This exposes the creamy cap of fat for crisping up.

Sprinkle the meat with sea salt just before grilling. Cook the goat slowly, brushing with generous amounts of chimichurri rojo as you turn the skewers. Cook until the internal temperature of the thickest slices reaches 130°F (55°C). The pieces shown here took 25–30 minutes. If necessary, give the meat a little extra crispness by moving it over the coals, but watch out for the fat flaring up like a hawk!

Roast the bell (sweet) peppers for a few minues until slightly blistered and charred.

Cut crispy slices off the outside of the meat and serve with a nice green salad and the roasted peppers. A real feast.

BARBECUE GOAT PICANHA WITH CHIMICHURRI ROJO

89

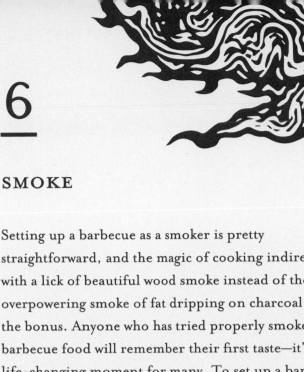

6

SMOKE

Setting up a barbecue as a smoker is pretty straightforward, and the magic of cooking indirect with a lick of beautiful wood smoke instead of the overpowering smoke of fat dripping on charcoal is the bonus. Anyone who has tried properly smoked barbecue food will remember their first taste—it's a life-changing moment for many. To set up a barbecue for indirect cooking and smoking, you simply place the coals on one side of the barbecue and the food on the other, and make sure the lid is on. This can be achieved simply using a standard kettle barbecue, or with a water pan or baffle plate. An offset smoker works like this anyway because it has a firebox attached to the side. A bullet or water smoker achieves this with a water pan, while a pellet grill is specially designed for indirect cooking. For simplicity, the instructions given for the recipes in this chapter assume you are using a typical kettle barbecue with the lid on for smoking.

+

GRILL TIPS

For the barbecue dry rub, I opted for a homemade version. Barbecuers have come up with some awesome ideas for covering Scotch eggs, including mixing panko breadcrumbs with a dry rub, as well as wrapping with bacon. What you decide to do for the dry coating is where you can transform these Scotch eggs into something uniquely yours.

Barbecue Scotch Eggs

RECOMMENDED HEAT:
Set up a barbecue for a little
gentle direct heat at 285°F
(140°C) with the lid on to crisp
up the sausage meat. If you wish,
add a little hickory and cherry
wood to smoke on the coals for
additional flavor and color.

MAKES 4

4 US extra-large (UK large)
   eggs
18oz (500g) good-quality
   sausage meat
3½oz (100g) black pudding
3 tbsp barbecue dry rub of
   your choice
Barbecue sauce of your choice,
   to glaze (optional)

Since posting my first recipe for barbecue Scotch eggs online about a year ago, the barbecue world has been going crazy for them. There have been some wonderful twists to the traditional recipe, with bacon-wrapped eggs becoming a firm favorite. My favorite tweak has been to add a sprinkle of black pudding on the inside with the sausage meat. This is definitely a super-food Scotch egg.

First, soft-boil the eggs. I have worked on the timings for eggs to achieve a perfect level of ooziness and found that simmering US large (UK medium)/US extra-large (UK large) hen's eggs for 6 minutes, then transferring them immediately to a bowl of iced water to cool works best for me. Once cooked, peel the eggs carefully.

For each Scotch egg, grab a handful of sausage meat and spread out into a disc on a piece of plastic wrap (clingfilm). Crumble over some black pudding until the sausage meat is evenly covered.

Place an egg on top and carefully bring the sausage meat over and around to cover the egg evenly, smoothing over the edges and joins.

Repeat for the remainder of the sausage meat and eggs, until you have four Scotch eggs. Let rest in the refrigerator for a minimum of 30 minutes–1 hour.

Just before cooking, sprinkle the eggs with the barbecue rub. This is where you can make a Scotch egg truly your own (see Grill Tips).

Smoke the Scotch eggs on the barbecue with the lid on for about 40 minutes. I added a little hickory and cherry wood to smoke for more flavor and color.

If you wish, brush the Scotch eggs all over with your choice of barbecue sauce, and cook for a minute or two more with the lid on, checking the sauce doesn't burn.

Ensure the sausage meat in the Scotch eggs reaches an internal temperature of 165°F (74°C) before serving.

Dirty Meat Battenburg

RECOMMENDED HEAT:
Set up a barbecue for indirect cooking at 250°F (120°C) with the lid on, adding some chunks of cherry wood to smoke on the coals, if you wish. .

SERVES 6

16 slices long-cut streaky bacon

18oz (500g) black pudding chubb (about 6 inches/15cm long)

18oz (500g) sausage meat

3 tbsp barbecue dry rub of your choice

Barbecue sauce of your choice, to glaze (optional)

What crazed individual dreamt up something as filthy as a Battenburg made of meat? Well, there have been a few examples recently, and this is my Dirty version: made into a barbecue "fatty" wrapped in bacon, with sausage meat and black pudding making up the two parts of the Dirty "Meatenburg." I always try to take my recipes up a gear if I can. I hope you like this one—it's filthily good and the leftovers make a great breakfast fry-up the next day!

This is a relatively easy fatty to assemble. Firstly, make a large bacon weave, using eight slices each way. A bacon weave is a way of turning thin strips of bacon into a flat surface for wrapping around other foods (see Grill Tips, right). Long-cut streaky bacon is best here, as it's much easier to wrap over.

Cut the 6-inch (15cm) long black pudding chubb into quarters lengthwise. Lay two of the quarters in the middle of the weave.

Add about the same length of sausage meat alongside the black pudding.

Alternate the remaining black pudding and sausage meat to create the next level, placing the black pudding on top of the sausage meat, and vice versa.

Pull the edges of the bacon weave across the meat, pull into a tight fat sausage shape, and tuck in any loose ends. Wrap in foil (like a Christmas cracker) and pop in the refrigerator to set for an hour. Remove from the refrigerator about an hour before cooking to let come to room temperature.

Dust the meat with the dry rub, dusting nice and evenly, but not too thickly.

Pop the fatty on the barbecue with the lid on for a couple of hours until it reaches an internal temperature of 165°F (74°C) and is thoroughly cooked through.

If you wish, brush the fatty with your favorite barbecue sauce for the last 10 minutes or so of smoking, to allow the barbecue sauce to set.

Cut the fatty into thick slices and serve with a little more barbecue sauce on the side (if using).

+

GRILL TIPS

Lay eight slices of the bacon on a sheet of foil so that they line up and are touching each other lengthwise. Fold back alternate slices from the middle. Lay a slice of bacon across along the line, then fold back the slices you folded back initially. Repeat this with the alternate bacon slices that you didn't fold back, laying across another slice. Repeat these two steps once more (so you are left with four slices to weave into the other half). Work from the middle to the edge, to get a nice tidy weave. Once you reach the edge, weave the other half in the same manner.

DIRTY MEAT BATTENBURG

Barbecue Peach and Pork Balls

RECOMMENDED HEAT:
Set up a barbecue for moderate direct grilling on at 320–350°F (160–180°C) with the lid, adding a couple of chunks of cherry or maple wood to smoke on the coals.

SERVES 4

4 canned peach halves

1½lb (700g) good-quality sausage meat

8 slices streaky bacon, each cut in half lengthwise

4 tsp barbecue dry rub of your choice (such as CountryWoodSmoke House Rub)

4 tbsp barbecue sauce of your choice, to glaze

Peaches and pork make a great combination. I've come up with a few recipes that combine the two, but this is probably the simplest (I love simple barbecue recipes). Here, the sweetness of the peach is tempered by the cooking, so the balls are not as sweet as you might imagine—there are just some really nice flavors. It's very easy to knock up a batch of these balls, and this has become one of my go-to demo'ing dishes.

Cut each of the peach halves into quarters.

Use your fingers to press a golf-ball-sized chunk of sausage meat flat on a piece of plastic wrap (clingfilm). Lay a piece of peach on top, then pull the edges of the sausage meat over to cover the peach, using your fingers to mold the meat into a ball around the peach until it is completely covered.

Wrap a strip of streaky bacon a few times around the ball. Repeat with the remainder of the peach pieces, sausage meat, and bacon strips until you have 16 balls.

Dust the balls evenly with a little barbecue dry rub.

Pop the balls on the barbecue and cook direct with the lid on. Cook for 4–5 minutes, then turn the balls over, ensuring the bacon is crisping up and the sausage meat is cooking through. Grill the balls for a further 4–5 minutes, then brush all over with the barbecue sauce and cook for a minute or two more with the lid on, checking the sauce doesn't burn.

Ensure the sausage meat in the balls reaches an internal temperature of 165°F (74°C) before serving.

Pork Belly, Pear, and Wedges

RECOMMENDED HEAT:
Set up a barbecue for two-zone cooking with a moderate direct heat of 350–400°F (180–200°C). Add a couple of chunks of pear wood to the coals to give a gentle smoke.

SERVES 4

3lb 5oz (1.5kg) pork belly, skin-on and boneless

4 pears, cored and quartered

4 medium sweet potatoes, cut into thick wedges

6 sprigs of fresh thyme

12fl oz (330ml) ginger beer

Coarse sea salt and coarse black pepper

+

GRILL TIPS

If you have a sweet tooth, try drizzling a little runny honey over the pear and sweet potato wedges just before serving.

Fatty pork belly is often paired with something sweet and sharp—usually apple sauce, which can be bland. To fix this, I've gone for pears instead. I also wanted a filling side dish to go with the pork, and opted for sweet potato wedges. The thyme and ginger beer add further great flavors, bringing it all together. The dish is cooked in a cast-iron skillet or pan, with a gently fruity, pear-wood smoke.

Score the pork skin with a knife, pour boiling water over the skin, and dry with paper towels (this helps crackling to form). Rub a few pinches of sea salt into the skin and sprinkle a pinch onto the meat side.

Cook the pork belly, skin-side facing down, in the direct-heat side of the barbecue until the skin puffs up and goes crispy (about 20 minutes). Take care that the skin doesn't burn, especially as the fat starts to render. An increase in the amount of white smoke will tell you that the fat is rendering and dropping onto the charcoal, so this is the time to ensure the skin doesn't burn.

Once you have nice crackling, move the pork to the indirect-side of the barbecue and cook for a further 1½–2½ hours, with the lid down, at 350–400°F (180–200°C). The pork should be softening now and have an internal temperature of about 176°F (80°C).

Put the quartered pears and sweet potato wedges in a cast-iron skillet or pan, scatter over the thyme, and season. Pour over the ginger beer and place the pork belly on top of the pears and wedges.

Return to the barbecue and cook with the lid on for a further hour or so, ensuring the meat doesn't dry out—you should be left with a little sticky ginger-beer residue on the base of the skillet or pan.

When ready, the pork, pear and wedges should be soft. The pork needs an internal temperature of 194–201°F (90–94°C) and to probe like soft butter—the fat needs to render down so that the meat isn't tough.

To serve, cut the pork belly into four large chunks, arrange the pear and sweet potato on top, and drizzle with the juices from the pan.

Roast Pork with Crispy Crackling

RECOMMENDED HEAT:
Set up a barbecue for two-zone cooking at 320–350°F (160–180°C) with the lid on, adding a chunk of cherry or apple wood to the coals to give a gentle smoke.

SERVES 4–6

3½–4½lb (1.5–2kg) pork loin roasting joint, skin-on

Coarse sea salt and freshly ground black pepper

To serve:

Roast potatoes

Selection of green vegetables, such as green beans and zucchini (courgettes)

+

GRILL TIPS

You can cook wonderful roast potatoes over the direct-heat side of the barbecue. Simply parboil potatoes suitable for roasting on the stovetop indoors for about 10 minutes, or until softened. Place the potatoes in a baking tray, toss with a few tablespoons of hot vegetable oil, and sprinkle generously with coarse sea salt and black pepper. Cook direct over the charcoal until nice and crispy.

Smoking food low and slow is great for cooking large chunks of meat until they are tender and juicy, but usually means that you won't get good crackling on a chunk of pork. Well, there is a way to get the benefits of both, by going somewhere between direct and indirect heat. There is a wonderful place—just to the side of being direct—where the meat gets to see a glancing blow of heat, but doesn't drip fat onto the coals, causing a flare-up. This is a great way of cooking: you get a slow cook, and you also crisp up the meat and get wonderful crackling.

Dry off the skin of the pork with some paper towels, then rub in sea salt and black pepper to taste—try to get plenty into the scores of the skin.

Place the pork on the barbecue with the skin-side facing the lit charcoal—around 4–6 inches (10–15cm) away from the edge of the coals. Put the lid on the barbecue, but keep an eye on the skin to ensure it doesn't burn. The skin should start puffing up to form crackling. If it doesn't, then move the joint slightly closer to the charcoal, but be wary of burning the crackling. This is a type of temperature control: moving closer to the heat will get the crackling going quicker.

Once you have the crackling as you like it, move the pork away from the coals—approximately 8 inches (20cm) is ideal—and cook with the lid on for around 30–40 minutes until the internal temperature reaches 145°F (63°C) for medium and 160°F (71°C) for well done. Remove from the barbecue and let rest for 20–30 minutes.

Cut the pork into thick slices and serve with the roast potatoes and your choice of green vegetables.

ROAST PORK WITH CRISPY CRACKLING

Double Chuck Roll

RECOMMENDED HEAT:
Set up a barbecue for indirect cooking at 265–285°F (130–140°C) with the lid on, using a wood such as cherry, pecan, or oak to smoke on the coals—a couple of pieces will be enough to create a nice gentle smoke.

FEEDS A CROWD

13lb (6kg) chuck joint, cut in half

10 tbsp barbecue dry rub for beef (enough for an even covering)

Bottle of beer (such as an amber ale)

To serve:

Brioche rolls

Homemade coleslaw (see my recipe for Simple Coleslaw on page 131)

Barbecue sauce of your choice

Chuck is a much under-valued cut of beef, usually ending up as burgers or chuck (stewing) steak. The darling of the barbecue world is currently brisket—it's the pinnacle of barbecue, but also very tricky to cook right unless you have the perfect cut of meat. On the other hand, a chuck joint cooked on the barbecue is a lot more forgiving. It is the bovine equivalent of a pork butt, and perfect for pulled beef (I call it pit beef). Brisket can be a bit too stringy when pulled, so I prefer to use chuck. Chuck is also great sliced and pretty good value for money. Here I wanted to get the best out of a chuck joint by cutting it in half and cooking each piece to a different internal temperature: one pulled and one sliced.

Dust the two halves of the chuck joint with the dry rub and place on the barbecue with the lid on for around 4 hours.

Splash a large sheet of foil with beer (and drink the rest!), then wrap the two joints together in the foil to smoke.

Smoke for a further 5 hours, keeping an eye on the internal temperature of the meat. You need to do this because the two joints are treated differently from this point and cooked at different temperatures.

Take one of the joints to an internal temperature of 200°F (93°C), where a digital thermometer probe goes in like butter. This will be the sliced joint. Once a temperature of 200°F (93°C) is reached, remove the joint from the barbecue and wrap tightly in two more pieces of foil, then a thick towel, and rest for roughly 90 minutes.

Take the second joint, which will be pulled, to an internal temperature of 205°F (96°C) before removing from the barbecue and resting for about an hour wrapped in foil.

Slice the lower-temperature chuck joint and shred the higher-temperature joint with two forks.

To serve, slice the brioche rolls in half and pile with the sliced chuck, followed by the pulled chuck. Be as generous as you can. Then load up with the coleslaw and barbecue sauce.

+

GRILL TIPS

As far as dry rubs go for this dish, you can use your favorite beefy dry rub. I went for CountryWoodSmoke Mocha Rub, but 50/50 sea salt and coarse black pepper would be pretty awesome for this, too.

Chicken, Squash, Thyme, and Cider Tray Bake

RECOMMENDED HEAT:
Set up a barbecue for gentle direct cooking at 285°F (140°C) with the lid on, adding a few chunks of apple wood to smoke on the coals.

SERVES 1

2 chicken thighs or legs, bone-in and skin-on

2 slices fall (autumn) squash (such as Crown Prince), deseeded

1 apple, quartered

2 sprigs of fresh thyme

Couple of good splashes of medium cider

Salt and freshly ground black pepper

To serve:

Rustic bread

I first cooked this dish in a wonderful orchard in Herefordshire, England. I was tasked with coming up with an interesting main course using seasonal ingredients from the fall (autumn) and also had to include the client's cider. I had a beautiful Crown Prince squash that was perfect, and I teamed it with smoked chicken thighs, fragrant thyme, and a hearty amount of good cider. The dish came together so well, I had to include it in the book.

Season the chicken thighs to taste and smoke over gentle direct heat on a barbecue with the lid on. Crisp up the skin and cook until the meat reaches an internal temperature of 165°F (74°C). Cook the slices of squash alongside the chicken until caramelized and starting to soften.

Place the chicken, squash, and apple quarters in a cast-iron skillet or pan, or use a strong disposable foil tray. Tear the thyme over the chicken and squash and pour over the cider.

Return to the barbecue with the lid on and let reduce over the heat. The cider will thicken and coat the chicken and squash in around 10 minutes. If the cooking vessel gets too dry, add a little more cider, but not too much—you need to save some for the chef.

Add a final seasoning of salt and black pepper, to taste, and serve with chunks of rustic bread.

CHICKEN, SQUASH, THYME, AND CIDER TRAY BAKE

Chili Marmalade Glazed Chicken Lollipops

RECOMMENDED HEAT:
Set up a barbecue for two-zone cooking at 320–350°F (160–180°C) with the lid on. Adding a chunk of hickory wood to the coals gives a nice smoke, but cherry and apple wood are good, too.

SERVES 1–2

4 chicken drumsticks

2 tbsp CountryWoodSmoke Mocha Rub (or your favorite barbecue dry rub)

For the glaze:

2 tbsp sweet chili sauce (such as Linghams)

2 tbsp fine-cut orange marmalade

A chicken lollipop is a wondrous thing: a juicy, bite-size nugget of chicken-drumstick meat with its own built-in "handle." Here, I layer the drumsticks with some great flavor combinations that are a bit out of the ordinary— the mocha rub gives a rich chocolate, coffee-spiced background, the hickory smoke a lovely deep savoriness, and the chili marmalade glaze a slight sweet chili kick, with a little bitterness from the marmalade that works very nicely. Even a certain bear would love this recipe. "Lollipopping" a drumstick is a bit tricky, as you need to cut through the tendons and pull back the skin and muscle to expose the bone so it can act as a handle. But a small sharp knife will make this a lot easier and neater.

To prepare the chicken lollipops, cut through the tendons and gently pull back the skin and muscle of each drumstick to expose the bone and create a lollipop handle.

Dust the lollipops lightly and evenly with the dry rub.

Pop the lollipops on the barbecue and cook with the lid on. Turn/move the lollipops, as required, so they cook evenly and the skin crisps up. The lollipops should take around 30 minutes to reach an internal temperature of 140°F (60°C).

In a small bowl, mix together the chili sauce and marmalade to make the glaze.

Brush the glaze evenly over the lollipops with a glazing or pastry brush, then cook for a further 10 minutes, ensuring the chicken reaches an internal temperature of 165°F (74°C) throughout.

Serve and enjoy!

Brisket Pot Roast

RECOMMENDED HEAT:
Set up a barbecue for indirect cooking at 265°F (130°C) with the lid on, adding a few chunks of cherry and pecan wood to smoke on the coals for additional flavor and color.

SERVES 4

4½lb (2kg) rolled brisket

1 red onion, thinly sliced

2 garlic cloves, thinly sliced

6 tbsp beef rub (I used the wonderful Quiet Waters Farm Grass Fed Beef Rub)

2 cups (500ml) your favorite dark beer

Salt and freshly ground black pepper

To serve:

Brioche rolls, or mashed potato and steamed kale

As much as I love a proper full packer cut brisket, sometimes I don't fancy cooking a whole one, or just want an easier life. When you visit a butcher in the UK, they usually have a rolled brisket flat out on display, which is great when slow-cooked and braised in a nice liquid such as beer! I never thought to write this dish up as a recipe, as it's pretty straightforward. But I posted some pictures in the CountryWoodSmoke Facebook Group and lots of people asked for the recipe, so I guess it looked tempting.

I'm a big fan of the smoke–braise–dip method. You smoke until you're happy with the bark (the crust around the outside); braise in a suitable container, with a braising liquid of your choice, such as stock or booze (beer or wine); then dip the cooked sliced brisket in the braising liquor when serving. I find a good ale works well with darker cuts of beef, such as brisket, short ribs, and cheek. A friendly chap called Jonathon from Black Tor Brewery on the edge of Dartmoor, in England, gave me a few bottles of his ales to see what I could come up with.

Place the brisket flat on a bed of the onion and garlic in a small baking pan (tin). Season the meat with the beef rub to add a lovely depth of flavor to the pot roast and gravy.

Smoke the brisket on the barbecue with the lid on for about 5 hours.

After 5 hours, pour half the beer over the brisket—enjoy the other half as a Pitboss perk—and then wrap up snugly with foil.

Cook for a further 4 hours or so, at 265°F (130°C), until the internal temperature of the brisket reaches 205°F (96°C) and the meat is soft like butter when probed.

Remove the brisket from the barbecue, cover the baking pan with foil, and let rest for around 30 minutes in the braising liquor. Season the liquor with salt and black pepper to taste.

Cut the meat into thick slices. Cut the brioche rolls in half, fill with generous helpings of meat, and enjoy as a sandwich, dunking into the braising liquor as a nice French dip. Alternatively, serve the sliced meat as a meal with some mashed potato and steamed kale, drizzled with the braising liquor, which will go down a treat.

BRISKET POT ROAST

Pulled Turkey with Alabama White Sauce

RECOMMENDED HEAT:
Set up a barbecue for indirect cooking at 285°F (140°C) with the lid on, adding some chunks of cherry wood to the coals to give a nice smoke.

SERVES 4

1lb 10oz–2¼lb (750g–1kg) turkey thigh joint, bone-in and skin-on (you don't need to be exact with weight, because you are cooking to temperature rather than time)

Barbecue dry rub of your choice (one that goes well with pulled pork is ideal)

For the Alabama white sauce:

6 tbsp good-quality mayonnaise

3 tbsp cider vinegar

1 tbsp American yellow mustard

1 tsp white sugar

1 garlic clove, mashed to a pulp

1 tsp creamed horseradish

Good pinch of sea salt and coarsely ground black pepper

To serve:

Brioche rolls

Rainbow slaw

Pickled gherkins

For many people, turkey is only served once a year, but I'm a big fan of this meat at any time. Away from the festive season, it provides tasty, good-quality meat, which, if cooked well with a lick of smoke, bears no resemblance to the cardboard turkey of many festive meals. Turkey thighs are even better value for money than the white meat. I love them—they pull so well, and should be on everyone's smoker. I went for some lovely cherry smoke to give the meat a nice pink smoke ring and a sweet smoked taste. A smoke ring is a slightly pink ring that forms on the edge of smoked meats in a complex interaction of the meat and smoke/combustion gases. The Alabama white sauce is awesome, especially on smoked turkey and chicken.

Dust the turkey thigh with the dry rub.

Smoke the turkey indirectly in the barbecue with the lid on for around 4–5 hours, until the internal temperature of the meat reaches 176°F (80°C). There's no need to take the temperature as high as you do for pulled pork, as turkey doesn't have the same collagen to break down to allow it to be pulled apart.

While the thigh is smoking, make a batch of Alabama white sauce. In a bowl, mix together the mayonnaise, cider vinegar, American mustard, white sugar, garlic, creamed horseradish, and sea salt and coarse black pepper. Set aside.

Once the turkey is cooked, use two forks to pull the meat apart.

Slice each brioche roll in half, toast lightly on the barbecue, and then load up with the rainbow slaw and pulled turkey. Drizzle with the Alabama white sauce and finish with a pickled gherkin each.

PULLED TURKEY WITH ALABAMA WHITE SAUCE

Slow-smoked Lamb Rack with Chimichurri Rojo

RECOMMENDED HEAT:
Set up a barbecue for indirect cooking at 285–320°F (140–160°C) with the lid on, adding a few chunks of olive wood to the coals for a nice gentle heat and toasty smoke.

SERVES 4

3lb 5oz (1.5kg) rack of lamb (you don't need to be exact with weight, because you are cooking to temperature rather than time)

Coarse sea salt and freshly ground black pepper

For the chimichurri rojo:

2 garlic cloves

½ red onion

Handful each of fresh flat-leaf parsley and oregano

About ½ cup (125ml) olive oil

1 tbsp tomato paste (purée)

Pinch of smoked paprika

Splash of red wine vinegar

Good pinch of coarse sea salt

To serve:

4 medium sweet potatoes

4 large flat mushrooms

Handful of grilled scallions (spring onions)

Lamb and fire go together perfectly, using either the searing heat of a charcoal grill or the gentle asado lick of heat and smoke of a nearby fire. I wanted to recreate a little of the asado style here on a plump little rack of lamb, so that it would be cooked gently, but have crisp smoky fat as a result of the proximity of the flames of a real wood fire. I picked up the rack of lamb from a local meat-box delivery company who had sourced it locally and it was excellent quality. The olive wood used for smoking here is great, giving off a gentle heat with a lovely toasty smoke.

To make the chimichurri rojo, blitz all the ingredients in a food processor or using a hand blender until you have a smooth-ish paste. If you wish, loosen the paste with a little more olive oil. Set aside.

Season the rack of lamb with sea salt and black pepper, to taste. Pop the rack on the barbecue next to the flame, but not directly over it. Cook gently with the lid on for about an hour. The fat will start to crisp up, but check the internal temperature of the thickest part of the meat reaches 130°F (55°C). Make sure to turn the rack around every 10 minutes, so the lamb cooks through evenly.

Brush the chimichurri over the lamb in the final stages of the cook—about 5 minutes before the end of the cook is fine.

While the lamb is cooking, put some sweet potatoes wrapped in foil directly onto the coals and cook, turning occasionally, until soft—this should take about 40 minutes.

Clean the mushrooms thoroughly, brush both sides with some chimichurri rojo, and grill over direct heat for a few minutes on each side until cooked through.

Grilled mushrooms are delicious with lamb. I had stumbled across a large giant puffball mushroom while out on a walk. I cut this into thick, cream-colored slices, which I grilled over direct heat and ate with the lamb. Remember: you have to be 100 per cent sure you have correctly identified any mushrooms you forage in the wild to avoid risk of poisoning.

Cook the scallions (spring onions) directly in the embers of the olive wood until charred and soft.

Once the lamb has cooked, remove from the heat, cover with foil, and rest for 20–30 minutes. Cut the lamb into thick, blushing cutlets and brush with some more chimichurri rojo. Serve the lamb on a large platter with the mushrooms, scallions, and sweet potatoes.

SLOW-SMOKED LAMB RACK WITH CHIMICHURRI ROJO

7

WOOD-FIRED OVENS

Cooking in a wood-fired oven is a very traditional way of cooking—the heat and food are in close proximity. You can either cook with a raging flame or use radiant heat after the fire has been taken out. Traditional brick and cobb ovens have a large thermal mass and can take hours to warm up. However, there is now a range of more modern wood-fired ovens available that are ready to cook at 750°F (400°C) in 20 minutes. There are also relatively lightweight versions of these, which can be taken to the beach or park. If you don't have a wood-fired oven, all the recipes in this chapter can also be cooked on a barbecue with a lid, although it may take longer.

Mocha Skirt Steak Fajitas

RECOMMENDED HEAT:
Heat a wood-fired oven or barbecue to a temperature of 660°F (350°C).

SERVES 4

2¼lb (1kg) skirt steak

3–4 tbsp dry rub (such as CountryWoodSmoke Mocha Rub or Fajita Rub)

1 red, green, and orange bell (sweet) pepper, cored, deseeded, and roughly sliced

1 red onion, thinly sliced

To serve:

Tortillas

1½ cups (200g) freshly grated Monterey Jack cheese

About 1 cup (200ml) sour cream

Cilantro (fresh coriander) leaves or sorrel

About 1 cup (250ml) guacamole

Chili sauce

Ever since I first had a play with a wood-fired oven, I'd wanted to cook a nice steak in one. My wife loves steak fajitas, so, of course, I wanted to come up with a recipe she would love. I had a lovely piece of skirt steak left over from a recent barbecue demo, which proved perfect for these fajitas. I cooked the steak in a pellet-powered wood-fired oven, which can reach up to 750°F (400°C) in under 20 minutes, and used a cast-iron steak sizzler pan. This dish has a fantastic flavor—the mocha rub flavors of coffee, chocolate, cumin, and chipotle work so well on the seared skirt steak.

Sprinkle the skirt steak generously with the dry rub, then let the meat sit for an hour at room temperature.

Meanwhile, char up the bell (sweet) peppers and onion in a cast-iron sizzler pan in the wood-fired oven or on the barbecue.

Once the edges of the vegetables are nicely charred, place the steak on top and cook for 5–6 minutes on each side, turning and flipping to ensure the meat is seared. The steak will be medium rare after this length of time, with an internal temperature of 130°F (55°C). This type of steak will toughen up if it is cooked past medium.

Slice the steak thinly across the grain and serve on tortillas with the charred vegetables, a little grated Monterey jack cheese, sour cream, cilantro (fresh coriander) leaves, and guacamole.

+

GRILL TIPS

You can try adding other ingredients to the finished tortillas, such as a nice pico de gallo. This is a Mexican side dish made from freshly chopped tomatoes, onion, cilantro (fresh coriander), salt, Serrano chili peppers, and lime juice.

MOCHA SKIRT STEAK FAJITAS

115

Glazed Salmon on Birch Bark

RECOMMENDED HEAT:
Heat a wood-fired oven
or barbecue with a lid to a
temperature of 350–400°F
(180–200°C).

SERVES 4

18oz (500g) salmon fillet,
skin-on

4 slices of fresh lemon

Salt and freshly ground black
pepper

For the glaze

3 tbsp runny honey

3 tbsp Pimm's Blackberry and
Elderflower

Plank cooking is a wonderful way of cooking delicate pieces of fish such as a salmon fillet. It protects the fish and stops it sticking, while also adding a wonderful smoky element. I sometimes find a plank to be too solid, but a sliver of silver-birch bark is a great alternative—it's thinner and so transmits heat better to the underside of the fish. The edges char and smolder more easily and you also get a lovely smoke from the silver birch.

Soak the silver-birch bark thoroughly in water for at least a couple of hours (this makes it less likely to catch fire). There is still a danger of it catching fire if it dries out, but a squirt of water from a water spray bottle will soon kill any flame.

Place the salmon fillet on the soaked silver-birch bark, with the skin-side facing down. Season to taste with salt and black pepper, and add the slices of lemon on top.

Pop the salmon—still on the piece of bark—in the wood-fired oven, or in a barbecue with the lid on, for around 20 minutes, until the internal temperature of the fish reaches 145°F (63°C).

To make the glaze, mix together the honey and Pimm's Blackberry and Elderflower in a bowl.

Glaze the salmon during the last 5 minutes of the cook to add just a little sweetness.

+

GRILL TIPS

For the glaze in this recipe, I used a 50:50 mix of honey and Pimm's Blackberry and Elderflower, which works really nicely with salmon. Other great mixes to try are 50:50 maple syrup and bourbon, or perhaps honey and Scotch whisky.

Wood-fired Rainbow Trout

RECOMMENDED HEAT:
Heat a wood-fired oven to a temperature of 400°F (200°C) or a barbecue with a lid to 350–400°F (180–200°C). If you're using a barbecue, set this up for indirect cooking.

SERVES 4–6

2 whole rainbow trout (or other suitable fish, such as sea bass or sea bream), gutted

1 lemon or lime, sliced into semi-circles

Sea salt and freshly ground black pepper

To serve:

Boiled new potatoes

Green salad

I've been fly-fishing for trout since I was 13 years old, and have enjoyed many wonderful meals caught by my own hand. Now that I have kids of my own, I love teaching them how to catch and cook their own food; they really enjoy eating the fish we catch, too. We'd been out for a lovely family day with my dad, and had caught two beautiful shiny specimens. When we got home, we lit the wood-fired oven using a pile of silver birch (my favorite wood to cook with) and roasted our catch—superb.

To stop the fish sticking to the pan or grill, slash the skin in a couple of places along the fillet, then push a slice of lemon or lime inside each slash. This lifts the skin proud of the cooking surface and stops the fish sticking.

Place the fish on a thick baking tray and season to taste with sea salt and black pepper. Please note: don't use a thin baking tray because it will warp.

Cook the fish in the hot oven away from too much flame—the wood-fired oven should be just ticking over. If you're using a barbecue, cook with indirect heat and ensure the lid is on.

Cook the fish until the flesh turns opaque and the internal temperature reaches around 144°F (62°C)—the skin should be nice and crispy.

Serve the fish with some boiled new potatoes and a nice green salad.

Wood-fired Pizzas with Rosemary and Scamorza

RECOMMENDED HEAT:
Heat a wood-fired oven to
a temperature of 750–840°F
(400–450°C), or get a pizza
stone in a barbecue with a lid
as hot as possible.

MAKES 8

For the pizza bases:
2¼lb (1kg) 00 bread flour, plus
    extra for dusting
¼oz (7g) instant dry yeast
Generous 2½ cups (620ml)
    cold water
¾oz (20g) fine sea salt
1 tbsp finely chopped fresh
    rosemary leaves

For the pizza tomato sauce:
Generous ¾ cup (200ml)
    strained tomatoes (passata)
2 tbsp red pesto
2 tbsp extra-virgin olive oil

For the topping:
2 balls smoked scamorza cheese,
    thinly sliced

A chapter on wood-fired cooking wouldn't be complete without a pizza recipe. Pizza is a truly wonderful food, and this is a simple, but grown-up version, with lovely flavors from the rosemary dough and smoked scamorza topping. It is also an ideal opportunity for me to share the pizza dough recipe that has served me well for many years.

Start making the dough the night before you plan to cook. Add 18oz (500g) of the flour, the yeast, and water to a large mixing bowl and stir until well combined. Cover the bowl with plastic wrap (clingfilm) and leave overnight at room temperature.

A few hours before cooking, add the remaining 18oz (500g) of flour, the salt, and rosemary to the dough. Knead the dough, either by hand or using a food mixer with a dough hook, until silky smooth—this will take around 10 minutes. Cover the bowl with plastic wrap and let rise in a warm place for an hour until it doubles in size.

Split the dough into 8 equal-sized balls (each weighing around 7oz/200g). Place the balls on a baking tray or two dusted with flour. Cover with a clean dish towel and let rise again in a warm place for up to 2 hours.

To make the pizza tomato sauce, mix the strained tomatoes (passata), red pesto, and olive oil in a bowl.

Stretch out the balls of dough individually to make the pizza bases—try to get them nice and thin. Spread the tomato sauce thinly over the base of each pizza and top with the slices of smoked scamorza.

Bake the pizzas in the wood-fired oven, turning as required, for a couple of minutes until the base is cooked and the scamorza is browned and bubbling. If you're using a pizza stone in a barbecue with the lid on, the pizzas will take around 6–8 minutes to cook.

WOOD-FIRED PIZZAS WITH ROSEMARY AND SCAMORZA

Wood-fired Roast Lamb

RECOMMENDED HEAT:
Heat a wood-fired oven
or barbecue with a lid to a
temperature of 350°F (180°C)
and let the flames die back a little,
so you have a gentle fire. If you're
using a barbecue, set this up for
indirect cooking.

FEEDS A SMALL CROWD

4½lb–5½lb (2–2½kg) leg
  of lamb

Sprigs of fresh rosemary

1 garlic clove, cut into slivers

A few sprigs of fresh thyme

Coarse sea salt and freshly
  cracked black pepper

To serve:

New potatoes

Carrots

Olive oil

Fire and lamb go so well together—the wonderful fat on lamb crisps up beautifully like nothing else. In a wood-fired oven, the meat is in close proximity to the gentle flames of smoldering logs and a gentle smoke. Many people regard outdoor cooking as a specific type of cooking when, in fact, you can cook anything outdoors that you would cook indoors, but give it the added magic of smoke and fire. You can, for example, produce a roast dinner outdoors—it is, in fact, perfect cooked indirect on a barbecue with a lid or, as I have done here, in a wood-fired oven.

Use the tip of a sharp knife to pierce small holes in the skin on top of the lamb. Pop a sprig of rosemary and a sliver of garlic into alternate holes. Season the lamb to taste with sea salt and black pepper, then scatter with the thyme.

Pop the leg of lamb in a large roasting pan and transfer to the oven or barbecue. If you're using a barbecue, cook with indirect heat at the same temperature and ensure the lid is on. Cook the lamb for around 1½ hours. If the lamb looks as if it's crisping up too much, then cover with a sheet of foil to stop the skin burning.

Cook the lamb until the skin is crisp and the meat is how you like it. You are looking for an internal temperature of 145°F (63°C) for nice, medium, blushing lamb and 153°F (67°C) for medium to well cooked. If you would like your lamb more rare or well done, see the *Internal Temperature Guide* on page 13 for guidance. Remove the lamb from the oven or barbecue and let rest for about 30 minutes, lightly covered with foil, before serving.

While the lamb is resting, parboil the potatoes and carrots for about 8 minutes, either indoors on the stovetop or outdoors on a campfire or barbecue. Transfer to a separate roasting pan and rub in some olive oil. Roast the potatoes and carrots in the oven, or in the barbecue with the lid on—they need around 30 minutes.

Carve the lamb and serve with the roast potatoes and carrots.

WOOD-FIRED ROAST LAMB

123

Wood-fired Eggplant

RECOMMENDED HEAT:
Heat a wood-fired oven
or barbecue with a lid to a
temperature of 480–570°F
(250–300°C).

SERVES 2

1 eggplant (aubergine)
Olive oil
Coarse sea salt

+

GRILL TIPS

*There are so many things you can
do with an eggplant (aubergine)
cooked in this way—it makes a
great baba ganoush, for example.
I like to serve the eggplant split
open with all manner of good
things, such as a drizzle of tahini,
some sour cream and Sriracha
chili sauce, and a few jeweled
pomegranate seeds. You can also
serve the eggplant with a bowl of
charred vegetable couscous. This
really is a super way of enjoying
a simple fire-cooked eggplant.*

Eggplant (aubergine) has a real affinity with fire: the skin
chars and blisters, while the flesh inside softens and easily
takes on smoke from the charring skin. A fire-cooked
eggplant requires very little to be done to turn it into
something utterly delicious. In some ways, I feel as if
I've cheated calling this a recipe because it's so easy, but
boy does it taste good.

Cut the eggplant (aubergine) in half lengthwise and place, cut-side
facing down, in a cast-iron skillet or pan greased with a little olive
oil. There's no need to remove the stalk.

Use a sharp knife to score the top of the eggplant skin, season to
taste with sea salt, and drizzle with a little olive oil.

Cook the eggplant in the wood-fired oven, or barbecue with the lid
on, for around 15 minutes, or until the flesh is very soft and the skin
blistered and charred.

Wood-fired Rhubarb Crumble

RECOMMENDED HEAT:
Heat a wood-fired oven
or barbecue with a lid to a
temperature of 400°F (200°C).
If you're using a barbecue, set
this up for indirect cooking.

SERVES 2

4 sticks of rhubarb, trimmed
  of leaves

4 tbsp apple juice

2 tsp turbinado (demerara)
  sugar

Couple of handfuls of granola

To serve:

Plain (natural) yogurt,
  ice cream, or cream

Rhubarb crumble is normally made with stewed rhubarb, but this misses some great opportunities to caramelize the rhubarb and really get the best out of a classic dessert. In the searing heat of a wood-fired oven, the flavor quickly intensifies. A little toasted granola sprinkled over the top gives a nice crunch.

Cut the sticks of rhubarb down to size, so they all fit in your cast-iron skillet or pan. Pour in the apple juice and sprinkle over the sugar.

Cook the rhubarb in the wood-fired oven, or using indirect heat in a barbecue with the lid on, for around 10 minutes, or until the rhubarb is charred and soft.

Sprinkle over the granola and pop the skillet or pan back in the oven or barbecue for 4–5 minutes, or until the granola is nicely toasted.

Serve with your choice of yogurt, ice cream, or cream.

8

ON THE SIDE

The recipes in this chapter are those good things that will turn the main food into a wonderful meal. They don't need to be fancy. It is just nice to have some variety on your plate, and these are the cornerstones of a lovely, simple barbecue meal.

CountryWoodSmoke Bread

RECOMMENDED HEAT:
Heat a wood-fired oven, barbecue, or an indoor oven to 425°F (220°C).

SERVES 8

- 2¼lb (1kg) good-quality strong white bread flour
- 2¾ cups (650ml) cold water
- ¼oz (7g) instant dry yeast
- ¾oz (20g) fine sea salt
- 3 tbsp extra-virgin olive oil
- 2 sprigs of fresh rosemary, leaves stripped
- Coarse sea salt

When people visit my home for a barbecue, I like to have irresistibly good homemade bread on the table as well as piles of meat. For me it is one of the cornerstones of a good outdoor meal. This is an incredibly easy bread to make, and the flavor develops in the dough as it is left overnight, which means the yeast can get to work properly. I've found a focaccia-style loaf to be one of my favorites, especially where the olive oil crisps up the crust a little, and the rosemary and sea salt topping works so well, too.

The night before you want to bake, mix 18oz (500g) of the flour, the water, and yeast in a large bowl, and cover with an airtight lid or some plastic wrap (clingfilm). Leave overnight at room temperature.

The next day, add the remaining 18oz (500g) of flour and the fine sea salt. This is quite a wet dough and tricky to handle, so if possible use a dough hook in a food mixer to knead the dough for around 10 minutes, until it looks smooth and silky. Place the dough in a large bowl, cover, and let rise in a warm place for a couple of hours until it is around twice the size.

Drizzle half the olive oil over the base of a large baking tray. Pour in the dough, using a silicon scraper to remove all the dough from the bowl. Spread the dough out evenly in the tray.

Cover with plastic wrap or a damp dish towel and let rise for another hour. Using a finger, gently press down in a regular pattern over the surface of the dough—aim for a pattern of three or four dimples across by four or five dimples down the longer side of the tray.

Pop a few rosemary leaves into each dimple and sprinkle a couple of pinches of coarse sea salt over the top of the dough.

Bake the bread for 40 minutes until golden brown on top and properly cooked—tap the base of the loaf, it should sound hollow.

Drizzle the remaining olive oil over the top of the bread and let rest for an hour before serving, if you can resist.

Dirty Rice with Chargrilled Vegetables

RECOMMENDED HEAT:
Level bed of red-hot embers using best-quality lump charcoal or the embers of a hardwood fire (silver birch, for example). You can just grill the vegetables on the barbecue until charred and soft, but this doesn't have the same magic.

SERVES 4

For the dirty rice:

2–3 sprigs of fresh rosemary

1¼ cups (260g) of easy-cook, long-grain white rice

2½ cups (600ml) boiling water

Handful of fresh flat-leaf parsley or cilantro (fresh coriander), chopped

2 tsp barbecue dry rub of your choice

4 tbsp extra-virgin olive oil

2 tbsp lemon juice

Coarse sea salt and freshly cracked black pepper

For the chargrilled vegetables:

1 each red, orange, and green bell (sweet) peppers, cored and deseeded, but left whole

2 shallots, peeled

12 cherry tomatoes

Selection of vegetables (such as eggplant/aubergine, zucchini/courgette, and garlic)

1 lemon, cut in half

I really wanted to include my recipe for "dirty" rice because it pulls together many of the wonderful ways in which you can add great flavors to a simple dish. Cooking vegetables (and herbs) in embers intensifies their flavor. I find watching a variety of brightly colored vegetables charring and blistering in the heat of embers a wondrous thing. I also like to char off woody herbs with a piece of smoldering charcoal in a stone bowl—the flavors you get from different herbs as they toast and char is incredible. Thyme, bay, and rosemary are ideal. I use rosemary in this recipe, but please experiment and see which flavors you prefer. This side dish always works well with grilled meats, fish, and vegetables, and is packed full of flavor.

Chargrill all the vegetables and the lemon halves by placing them in the embers of the barbecue or hardwood fire, and cook until starting to char and soften up.

To make the dirty rice, place the sprigs of rosemary in a fireproof bowl—I like to use a stone bowl—and put a hot ember on top. Remove the ember once the rosemary is toasted and charred.

Cook the rice in a pan over a medium heat on the stovetop indoors, as per the directions on the packet—I use 2 mugs of boiling water per 1 mug of rice. (If you are feeling adventurous, you can, of course, cook the rice outdoors on the barbecue or campfire.)

Chop the charred vegetables and lemon, and add to the rice, along with the charred rosemary and chopped parsley or cilantro (fresh coriander). Add the barbecue dry rub, olive oil, and lemon juice. Season to taste with sea salt and black pepper, and mix everything together well.

Serve and enjoy. You should be able to taste the range of different flavors and have some lovely pops of flavor from the charred veg.

Simple Coleslaw

2–3 large carrots

½ celery root (celeriac)

½ small red cabbage

4 heaped tbsp good-quality
  mayonnaise

2 tsp American yellow mustard

4 tbsp lemon juice

Sea salt and freshly ground
  black pepper

In addition to good bread, I think you need something tangy to cut through rich fatty barbecue food—as a cornerstone to an outdoor feast. A simple coleslaw does the job perfectly and is always good to have at hand when you're throwing a barbecue. Homemade coleslaw is also fresh and not as creamy and gloopy as commercial coleslaw.

Peel and coarsely grate the carrots and celery root (celeriac). Finely slice the red cabbage into ribbons—get these as thin as you can. Mix the vegetables together in a large bowl.

Mix all the liquid ingredients together in a separate bowl, and then stir through the vegetables.

Season with sea salt and black pepper to taste—a pinch of each should be about right.

+

GRILL TIPS

There's a lot of different directions you can take a good coleslaw. Try changing things up with dessert apple or pear grated into the coleslaw.

Piccalilli Potato Salad

SERVES 4

18oz (500g) new potatoes

4 tbsp sour cream

1 tbsp each chopped fresh
   flat-leaf parsley and chives

3 tbsp piccalilli (British mustard
   pickle)

Sea salt and freshly ground
   black pepper

As much as I love the meat of a barbecue, I'm also a big fan of good side dishes, or fixin's as they're known in the US. Potato salad is up there as a classic for me, but I really don't like the commercial stuff in tubs with lots of gloopy sauce. I also love my potato salad to be a little warm. British piccalilli is a wonderful condiment, and a good brand will have that lovely mustardy twang and crunchy vegetables. I was looking for something to ramp up the flavor of my potato salad, and thought a little piccalilli would work a treat stirred in… and I was right.

Using either an outdoor grill or kitchen stovetop, cook the potatoes in a pan of slightly salted boiling water for about 10–12 minutes or until very tender. Drain in a colander and let cool slightly.

In a large bowl, mix the potatoes with the sour cream, chopped herbs, and piccalilli. Season to taste with sea salt and black pepper. Stir until everything is fully mixed.

Serve as a side at your barbecue—it is perfect with ribs or chunky pork chops—garnishing with an extra dollop of piccalilli and a few sprigs of flat-leaf parsley.

Grilled Cauliflower Steaks with Miso and Sesame Sauce

RECOMMENDED HEAT:
Set up a barbecue for moderate (320–350°F/160–180°C), direct cooking using lump charcoal.

SERVES 2

1 whole cauliflower, cut into 1¼-inch (3cm) thick slices across the stem

2 tbsp sesame oil

2 tbsp Togarashi spice mix

For the miso and sesame sauce:

2 tbsp miso paste (any color will do)

2 tbsp lemon juice

2 tbsp rice vinegar

1 tbsp toasted white sesame seeds

To serve:

Tamari soy sauce

Cauliflower is very much the in-vogue vegetable, which is not really surprising because its virtues have long been overlooked. I think cauliflower really shines when it picks up a sear and gentle caramelization from a barbecue grill. This toasts up the cauliflower, and the resulting flavor is sublime, especially when teamed with either a Middle Eastern flavor combo or something a little farther east, as I have gone for here. The savory umami hit of miso and sesame works spectacularly well, along with a little hit of Togarashi spices.

Combine all the ingredients for the sauce in a bowl and set aside.

Brush the slices of cauliflower with the sesame oil, then sprinkle with the Togarashi spice mix.

Grill the cauliflower slices, turning occasionally, for around 15–20 minutes, or until they start to soften and char.

Brush the slices on both sides with the miso and sesame sauce and cook for another few minutes on each side. The cauliflower should be soft and toasted, and smell amazing.

Serve with a bowl of tamari soy sauce, breaking off the cauliflower florets and dipping them into the sauce.

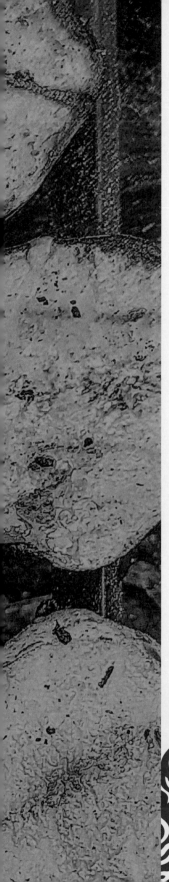

9

SWEET THINGS

A few sweet things and a few drinks to embellish your food. When you're sat tending a hot barbecue, you need some simple delights to make the experience as pleasurable as possible.

Grilled Pears with Honey

RECOMMENDED HEAT:
Red-hot grill using lump charcoal for some direct grilling action.

SERVES 2

2 pears (ideally, sweet Comice-style pears)

2 tbsp runny honey

To serve

Cream or plain (natural) yogurt

I wondered whether I would get this recipe past the book's editor, as it is ridiculously simple. However, it is so delicious that I just couldn't leave it out—I'm very glad I did include it. When I was writing this book, the pears in my garden were plentiful. Pears are at their best when charred slightly over direct heat, while the little drizzle of honey turns them into something that is almost like candied pear, but with smoke and char.

Cut each pear into four slices lengthwise (they don't need to be peeled first, nor cored).

Place the pear slices on the grill over direct heat to sear and caramelize. Sear one side first, then drizzle the slices evenly with honey before flipping and drizzling again on the other side—this should take a few minutes for each side.

You'll know when the pears are cooked because the flesh starts to soften and the honey caramelizes into a toffee-like crust.

The pears are perfect served with a little cream or yogurt.

RECOMMENDED HEAT:
Red-hot, good-quality lump
charcoal with a plancha/griddle
plate or grill.

SERVES 4

Whole pineapple, peeled,
halved, cored, and cut
into slices (about ⅔ inch/
15mm thick)

Brown sugar (optional)

Maple butter (available at
grocery stores or online)

Plancha Pineapple with Charcoal-melted Maple Butter

A thick slice of juicy charred pineapple on a red-hot plancha, with a spoonful of sweet maple butter swiftly placed on top, and a chunk of red-hot lump charcoal sizzling and searing the maple butter to coat the pineapple. This recipe is a real sweetie, and also has that added theatrical flourish which I think takes barbecues to another wonderful level.

Caramelize the pineapple slices on the red-hot plancha/griddle plate or grill. A small sprinkling of brown sugar can help if the pineapple is not caramelizing enough. Cook the pineapple for 4–5 minutes on each side, until nicely brown and soft.

Put 1 teaspoon of maple butter on top of each slice of pineapple, then place a lump of red-hot lump charcoal on top of the butter. This will sizzle, melt, and caramelize the butter on top of the pineapple.

Take the pineapple to the table with the charcoal still sizzling on top and serve this dessert with a dramatic flourish.

Barbecue Chili Chocolate Brownies

RECOMMENDED HEAT:
Set up a barbecue for indirect cooking at 350–400°F (180–200°C), adding a chunk of cherry wood to the coals for a gentle smoke.

MAKES 20

2 cups (400g) unbleached superfine (golden caster) sugar

2 sticks (225g) unsalted butter, melted

About ½ cup (60g) good-quality cocoa powder

1 ancho chili pepper, soaked in warm water until soft, then drained and finely chopped

1 tsp vanilla extract

4 US extra large (UK large) eggs

1¾ cups (225g) all-purpose (plain) flour

½ tsp baking powder

Pinch of fine sea salt

Brownies are such simple things to cook on a barbecue, and this recipe is really easy. The ancho chili pepper works so well with the chocolate in these brownies. Ancho chilis (dried poblano peppers) are fruity, smoky, and not too hot. It is definitely worth adding the chunk of cherry wood to get a very light, sweet-cherry smoke.

Line a rectangular baking pan (tin), measuring approximately 13 x 9 inches (33 x 23cm), with baking paper.

Mix all the ingredients together in a large bowl, adding them in the order they appear in the ingredients list and folding in each time you add a new ingredient.

Pour the brownie mixture into the lined baking pan. Pop in the barbecue for around 25 minutes, until the mixture is just set. You don't want the brownies to be too overcooked, as the centers should be a bit soft and fudgy.

Once cooled slightly, cut into squares while in the baking pan—cutting four lines by five gives 20 lovely chili brownies.

Smoky Tomato Bloody Mary

RECOMMENDED HEAT:
Set up a barbecue for moderate (320–350°F/160–180°C), direct grilling, adding a small handful of hickory wood chips to the coals to smoke.

MAKES 2

Handful of ripe cherry tomatoes

1¼ cups (300ml) tomato juice

Couple of good dashes of Worcestershire sauce

Good dash of chipotle Tabasco

2 tsp barbecue dry rub of your choice (I used CountryWoodSmoke House Rub), plus extra for the decorative rim

Juice of ½ lemon

Generous ⅓ cup (100ml) vodka

Handful of ice cubes, plus extra to serve

To serve:

2 celery sticks

2 fresh lemon wheels

Grilling and smoking tomatoes to add to a Bloody Mary gives the cocktail a lovely hint of hickory smoke. The caramelized tomato adds a rich dimension to the drink. The magic of fire and smoke works so well here, and the small amount of dry rub makes this a barbecue drink to get you going for those early morning smoking sessions.

Place the cherry tomatoes on the moderately hot grill and cook until charred and smoky. Let cool.

In a food processor or using a hand blender, blitz together the grilled smoky tomatoes with the tomato juice, Worcestershire sauce, Tabasco, barbecue dry rub, and lemon juice. You can adjust the quantities given here to suit your taste, but these work well for me. Chill the drink in the refrigerator for an hour.

Remove the drink from the refrigerator. Add the tomato juice mixture, vodka, and a handful of ice cubes to a cocktail shaker or pitcher (jug). Shake or stir until chilled.

To make a decorative rim for each glass, sprinkle the extra dry rub on a plate. Dip the rims of the glasses in some water and then in the rub.

Strain the Bloody Marys into the glasses. If you're using a pitcher, and don't have a cocktail strainer, use a sieve to strain the drink into the glasses.

Add a couple of ice cubes to each glass. Stir each drink with a celery stick, then leave this in the glass. Garnish the rim of each glass with a lemon wheel, sit back, and enjoy.

Grilled Lime CoronaRita

RECOMMENDED HEAT:
Hot grill using lump charcoal.

MAKES 2

2 limes

2–3 tsp turbinado (demerara) sugar

Lots of ice cubes

1⅔ cup (400ml) Margarita Mix (such as Jose Cuervo)

4 shots (generous ⅓ cup/ 100ml) tequila (be as generous as you dare)

2 Coronita (mini-sized bottle of Corona)

It's hot work tending a grill and cooking for people, and one of the most important rules is to make sure you keep well hydrated. This super-sized cocktail guarantees this for sure. Grilling the limes gives a lovely caramel edge to their already wonderful flavor (I'm a big fan of limes). You'll need a clip-on Corona bottle-holder for each cocktail, which you can buy online. The upside down Coronita bottle glugs down, as you drink the cocktail, making the drink even more refreshing—a beer cocktail… what's not to like?

Cut one of the limes into thick slices and halve the other one. Sprinkle the cut-sides of the sliced limes with the turbinado (demerara) sugar, then grill over a high heat to caramelize. Let cool.

Fill a powerful high-speed blender three-quarters full with ice cubes. Pour in the Margarita Mix and the tequila shots, and squeeze in the juice of the two lime halves. Blend the drink until it is smooth and slushy.

Pour the slushy drink into a couple of margarita glasses or if, like me, you are very dehydrated, then one very, very large glass...

Clip the Corona bottle-holders to the sides of the glasses to hold the Coronita bottles in place. Open the bottles and quickly insert one upside down in the clip on each glass.

To serve, dice the grilled lime slices, reserving one for the side of each glass. Sprinkle the sliced lime over the top of the slushy drinks. Pop a straw in each glass, and enjoy!

Index

Acknowledgments

I have to start by thanking my awesome wife, Lisa. She has been my rock, who has always encouraged, loved, and supported me, while keeping the kids looked after so I could crack on with cooking and writing. The mountains of washing up produced by all this cooking have always disappeared. Thank you, my love.

Thank you to my chief tasting team, my 3 wonderful children, Rory, Elsie, and Louie. Your feedback and input into my food is always appreciated with love.

Thank you to my parents; Dad, you are my hero, and Mum, I miss you.

To all my dear friends, I am so fortunate to have you in my life; to be able to share the food from my grill with you. For me, when I cook for you, I am showing that I care for you.

Thank you to all my friends within the global BBQ community. I always say BBQ people are the best people—you love what you do, you feed so many, and tirelessly work to get the word out about how wonderful BBQ is. Big, smoky love to the BBQ family—the world is a better place because of BBQ and because of you.

To those who have attended classes at my UK BBQ School in Devon, seeing your faces as you enjoy the food we create together, and the excitement when you cook your own BBQ masterpieces, is a real joy to behold.

Thank you to my superstar agent, Robert Gwyn-Palmer. Your patience and constant upbeat enthusiasm kept me going, even when I thought this book would never happen. Thank you for believing in me.

Thank you to all at Ryland Peters & Small and the Dog 'n' Bone team for having the vision to see the potential in this book. Pete, Caroline, Cindy, and Eoghan, you have helped me bring my dream to fruition, thank you so much.

Thanks to the businesses I work with, who support what I do at CountryWoodSmoke, including all the butchers, BBQ companies, rub and sauce makers, and those at Alfresco Chef, who have helped me to get my BBQ rubs to market. Thanks also to the retailers who are stocking this book. It's an exciting time for UK BBQ and I am enjoying sharing the ride with you.

My photographer friends—Nick Hook, Richard Budd, and Matt Austin—thank you for kindly letting me use some of your beautiful pictures. I am always inspired seeing what you create. Thank you to James Brooks and his team of creative geniuses, you help to turn my BBQ dreams into wonderful videos that support this project.

Thank you to the following for your inspiration and encouragement along my journey: Dan Toombs, Genevieve Taylor, Jon Finch, Ben Merrington, DJ BBQ (aka Christian Stevenson), Dr Sweetsmoke, and Richard Holden.

"BARBECUE MAY NOT BE THE ROAD TO WORLD PEACE, BUT IT'S A START."
Anthony Bourdain, RIP

You can learn more about Marcus, read what he's been cooking with fire, and sample more of his delicious recipes at the following places:

www.countrywoodsmoke.com
www.ukbbqmag.com
www.ukbbqschool.com
Twitter: @devonwoodsmoke
Instagram: @countrywoodsmoke